Choice Theory: A Very Short Introduction

VERY SHORT INTRODUCTIONS are for anyone wanting a stimulating and accessible way into a new subject. They are written by experts, and have been translated into more than 45 different languages.

The series began in 1995, and now covers a wide variety of topics in every discipline. The VSI library now contains over 500 volumes—a Very Short Introduction to everything from Psychology and Philosophy of Science to American History and Relativity—and continues to grow in every subject area.

Titles in the series include the following:

AFRICAN HISTORY John Parker and
    Richard Rathbone
AMERICAN HISTORY Paul S. Boyer
AMERICAN LEGAL HISTORY
    G. Edward White
AMERICAN POLITICAL PARTIES
    AND ELECTIONS L. Sandy Maisel
AMERICAN POLITICS
    Richard M. Valelly
AMERICAN SLAVERY
    Heather Andrea Williams
ANARCHISM Colin Ward
ANCIENT EGYPT Ian Shaw
ANCIENT GREECE Paul Cartledge
ANCIENT PHILOSOPHY Julia Annas
ANCIENT WARFARE Harry Sidebottom
ANGLICANISM Mark Chapman
THE ANGLO-SAXON AGE John Blair
ANIMAL RIGHTS David DeGrazia
ARCHAEOLOGY Paul Bahn
ARISTOTLE Jonathan Barnes
ART HISTORY Dana Arnold
ART THEORY Cynthia Freeland
ATHEISM Julian Baggini
THE ATMOSPHERE Paul I. Palmer
AUGUSTINE Henry Chadwick
BACTERIA Sebastian G. B. Amyes
BEAUTY Roger Scruton
THE BIBLE John Riches
BLACK HOLES Katherine Blundell
BLOOD Chris Cooper
THE BRAIN Michael O'Shea
THE BRICS Andrew F. Cooper
BRITISH POLITICS Anthony Wright

BUDDHA Michael Carrithers
BUDDHISM Damien Keown
BUDDHIST ETHICS Damien Keown
CAPITALISM James Fulcher
CATHOLICISM Gerald O'Collins
THE CELTS Barry Cunliffe
CHOICE THEORY Michael Allingham
CHRISTIANITY Linda Woodhead
CIRCADIAN RHYTHMS Russell Foster
    and Leon Kreitzman
CITIZENSHIP Richard Bellamy
CLASSICAL MYTHOLOGY
    Helen Morales
CLASSICS Mary Beard and
    John Henderson
CLIMATE CHANGE Mark Maslin
THE COLD WAR Robert McMahon
COMMUNISM Leslie Holmes
CONSCIOUSNESS Susan Blackmore
CONTEMPORARY ART
    Julian Stallabrass
COSMOLOGY Peter Coles
THE CRUSADES Christopher Tyerman
DADA AND SURREALISM
    David Hopkins
DARWIN Jonathan Howard
THE DEAD SEA SCROLLS
    Timothy Lim
DECOLONIZATION Dane Kennedy
DEMOCRACY Bernard Crick
DESIGN John Heskett
DREAMING J. Allan Hobson
DRUGS Les Iversen
THE EARTH Martin Redfern

Michael Allingham

CHOICE THEORY

A Very Short Introduction

OXFORD
UNIVERSITY PRESS

OXFORD
UNIVERSITY PRESS

Great Clarendon Street, Oxford OX2 6DP

Oxford University Press is a department of the University of Oxford.
It furthers the University's objective of excellence in research, scholarship,
and education by publishing worldwide in

Oxford New York

Auckland Bangkok Buenos Aires Cape Town Chennai
Dar es Salaam Delhi Hong Kong Istanbul Karachi Kolkata
Kuala Lumpur Madrid Melbourne Mexico City Mumbai Nairobi
São Paulo Shanghai Taipei Tokyo Toronto

Oxford is a registered trade mark of Oxford University Press
in the UK and in certain other countries

Published in the United States
by Oxford University Press Inc., New York

© Michael Allingham 2002

British Library Cataloguing in Publication Data

Data available

Library of Congress Cataloging in Publication Data

Data available

ISBN 978-0-19-280303-0

Typeset by RefineCatch Ltd, Bungay, Suffolk
Printed and bound by
CPI Group (UK) Ltd, Croydon, CR0 4YY

Contents

Preface

Albert Einstein introduces his brilliant exposition, *Relativity*, in the following terms.

> The present book is intended, as far as possible, to give an exact insight into the theory of relativity to those readers who, from a general scientific and philosophical point of view, are interested in the theory, but who are not conversant with the mathematical apparatus of theoretical physics. The work presumes a standard of education corresponding to that of a university matriculation examination, and, despite the shortness of the book, a fair amount of patience and force of will on the part of the reader. The author has spared himself no pains in his endeavour to present the main ideas in the simplest and most intelligible form. ... May the book bring some one a few happy hours of suggestive thought!

Apart from substituting 'choice' for 'relativity' and 'logic' for 'physics' I can find no better way to express the aim of this book.

Choice theory explores the reasoning which underlies coherent patterns of choice: it explores what it means to act rationally. Why is this important? As Aristotle reminds us, 'the origin of action is choice, and that of choice is desire and reasoning ... good action and its opposite cannot exist without a combination of intellect and character'. Choice theory develops the intellectual reasoning which is necessary for good action: the character which is also necessary for this is up to you.

The book is short not because it covers a small territory, but because it does not go into exhaustive detail of the territory which it does cover. Many interesting sights are mentioned, but in many cases only incomplete directions are given for finding them: the book is more a guide than a gazetteer. Many arguments are missing, or only sketched: the reader may like to supply, or complete, these, and would do well to do so where this is suggested by phrases such as 'it is easy to see that'. The notes at the end of the book indicate where help may be found, and also warn of the ascents which even the more intrepid explorer might be unwise to attempt. A number of open questions and paradoxes are raised but not resolved, though guidelines which might help the reader find his own resolution are indicated: the reader must take his own views on such matters.

I am grateful to Shelley Cox of Oxford University Press for suggesting that I write this book and for commenting on the manuscript, and to those of my family and friends who too have provided comments. I am also grateful to the University of Siena for providing an ideal ambience in which to reflect on the underlying ideas, and to Magdalen College for giving me a period of leave in which to transform these into words.

List of illustrations

Chapter 1
Choice and desire

Choose life. Choose a job. Choose a career. Choose a family. Choose a
big television, choose washing machines, cars, compact disc players
and electrical tin openers. Choose good health, low cholesterol and
dental insurance. Choose fixed-interest mortgage repayments.
Choose a starter home. Choose your friends. Choose leisurewear and
matching luggage. Choose a three-piece suite on hire purchase . . .
Choose your future. Choose life.

But why should I want to do a thing like that? I chose not to choose
life: I chose something else. And the reasons? There are no reasons.
Who needs reasons?

Thus the opening voice-over of the film *Trainspotting*. But is
the speaker, one Renton, choosing rationally? His choice of
'something else' rather than 'life' is his concern: it may not be my
choice or yours, but it cannot, by itself, be irrational. *De gustibus
non disputandam est*, as they say. But his claiming to
have no reason is a different matter for, as language suggests and
as we shall see, there is an intimate connection between reason
and rationality. Indeed, Renton himself soon provides a
reason:

People think it's all about misery and desperation and death and all
that shite, which is not to be ignored, but what they forget – is the

pleasure of it. Otherwise we wouldn't do it. After all, we're not stupid. At least, we're not that stupid.

And, with an enviable practicality, he continues:

> When you're on junk you have only one worry: scoring. When you're off it you have to worry about all sorts of other shite. Got no money: can't get pished. Got money: drinking too much. Can't get a bird: no chance of a ride. Got a bird: too much hassle. You have to worry about bills, about food, about some football team that never wins, about human relationships and all the things that really don't matter.

All choices, just as Renton's, arise from both the heart and the head. The heart provides the passion and the head the reasons. Choices based on the most minute reasoning but lacking any desire are vacuous. But desire without reason is impotent: it is fit only for the enraged child who wants both to go home and not to go home.

1. *The Choice of Hercules*: Virtue versus Vice (Paolo de Matteis, 1712)

Aristotle (384–322 BCE), the founder of choice theory, and indeed of logic itself, identifies the connection. 'The origin of . . . choice is desire and reasoning with a view to an end – this is why choice cannot exist without . . . reason'; or, more concisely, 'choice is deliberate desire'. And David Hume (1711–76), that beacon of the Scottish Enlightenment, famously claims that 'reason is and ought only to be the slave of the passions'. Passions themselves, even Renton's, are neither reasonable nor unreasonable: 'a passion can never, in any sense, be called unreasonable'. Thus 'it is not contrary to reason to prefer the destruction of the whole world to the scratching of my finger; it is not contrary to reason for me to chuse my total ruin to prevent the least uneasiness of an Indian'.

A framework

Reasonableness is a property of patterns of choices, not of individual choices. There is nothing irrational in wanting to go home but there is something amiss in wanting both to go home and not to go home. There is nothing irrational in Renton's choosing heroin but his choice looks odd if he also chooses to avoid the possibility of misery, desperation, and death. Thus to explore what it means to be rational we must look at patterns of choices. We must look at the way in which choice changes when the menu changes. This framework of menus and choices needs some explanation.

By a *menu* I mean a list of items from which choice must be made. (Technical terms, such as 'menu', italicized when they first appear, are explained in the glossary at the end of the book.) But unlike a restaurant menu a menu in our sense is set out in such a way that something must be chosen. A simple restaurant menu might be

Sandwiches
Avocado
Bacon

3

This would allow the replete to choose nothing, and the hungry to choose both. The corresponding menu in our sense would be

Items
Nothing
Avocado alone
Bacon alone
Both

MENU

Potage à la Brunoise.

Saumon à la Tartare.   Saumon en aspic.
Saumon à la Montpellier.   Mayonnaise de saumon.
Coquille de crabe.   Filets de soles en aspic.
            Anguilles en aspic.

            Salade.   Homard en salade.
Poulets rôtis. Poulets à la Béchamel. Mayonnaise de poulet.
        Poulet en aspic.   Cānetons rôtis.
Agneau rôti.   Rosbif farci.   Galantine de veau.
                Paons rôtis.
        Côtelettes d'agneau aux petits pois.
        Côtelettes d'agneau aux tomates.
Galantine de poulet.   Langues de bœuf.
Chaudfroid de cailles.   Chaudfroid de pigeons.
Pompinettes à l'Italienne.   Foie gras en aspic.
Ris de veau en aspic.   Quenelles de veau en aspic.
Sandwiches aux anchois.   Sandwiches au cresson.
            Sandwiches aux œufs.

Gelées à l'eau de vie de Dantzic.   Gelées à la Belgrave.
    Gelées au curaçoa.   Gelées au punch.
Macedoine de fruits en gelée.   Gelées au marasquin.
Crème de limon.   Crème à la vanille.   Crème aux pistaches.
            Crème à l'ananas.
    Meringues.   Franchinettes.   Blancmanges.
Pâtisserie à la Française.   Pâtisserie à la Chantilly.
Gâteaux à la Neapolitaine.   Gâteaux aux abricots.
    Compôte de poires.   Compôte d'ananas.
    Compôte d'abricots.   Compôte de pêches.
    Chartreuse d'oranges.   Chartreuse de fraises
    Chartreuse d'abricots.   Chartreuse de pêches.
        Tipsy cake.   Petits nougats.
            Tartelettes à la mosaïque.

Floreat Magdalena

2. A menu: Magdalen College, 24 June 1889

4

Now, by construction, some item must be chosen, even if that item is the one labelled 'Nothing'. (To emphasize that they are not to be taken literally, menus and menu items are either given initial capitals or placed inside quotation marks.) However, we must allow for ties, that is, for more than one item to be chosen jointly. For example, Avocado alone may tie with Bacon alone. To say that these two items tie, or are chosen jointly, is just to say that we are equally content with either. It does not mean that we consume both: in the face of a tie you may imagine that we rely on some arbitrary tie-breaker, such as tossing a coin, and then consume the winner. Without this artificial device we could find ourselves in the same position as Buridan's ass, the creature of the scholastic philosopher Jean Buridan (1295–1358). This unfortunate animal, placed midway between two identical bales of hay, starved to death because he had no reason for moving one way rather than the other.

As an illustration of the way in which rationality may be found, or not found, in patterns of choices consider the Sandwich menu. Faced with this you choose Avocado; there can be nothing irrational in this. However, when the waiter arrives to take your order he tells you that Cheese is also available. The effect of this is that you now have a three-item menu: Avocado, Bacon, and Cheese. You choose Bacon. Again, there can be nothing irrational in this individual choice. But there is clearly something untoward in your pattern of choices: your choice changes when the menu is enlarged by the addition of something which you do not want, namely Cheese.

I shall throughout the book assume that there are sufficient items for the problem not to be trivial; for example, I shall ignore menus which consist of only one item. I shall also, except where this cannot be avoided, assume that all menus are finite. This latter assumption rules out two classes of choices. An example of the first class is that of choosing a number of dollars, without restriction. The problem here is that there are infinitely many discrete amounts: $1, $2, $3, and so forth. This class can be ruled out without qualm as almost all

5

interesting choice menus have some 'upper' and 'lower' limits. An example of the second class is that of choosing the temperature of a bath, say within the range 10 to 60 degrees centigrade. Here the menu obviously has an upper and a lower limit, but the temperature can vary continuously between these. Ruling out this class causes no practical problems. We lose nothing of substance if we restrict our choice to temperatures which vary in increments of, say, 0.1 degrees. If we do this our menu has only a finite number of items.

In addition, I shall, in the main, assume that choice is timeless. This is not as restrictive as it may seem as most choices involving time can be expressed in a timeless way. For example, you can commit yourself today to choosing 'Avocado today and Bacon tomorrow', which is clearly a choice involving time. You can also commit yourself today to choosing 'Bacon tomorrow if it is raining tomorrow, or if Pegasus wins the Derby, or if I have chosen Bacon today'. In each of these examples time enters the picture only in an inessential way. However, as we shall see, not all choices fit this pattern.

Some settings

In the remainder of the book I explore what it means to choose rationally in various settings. I start by exploring reason and rationality in the simplest context, that where menus consist of definite items, such as Avocado and $100. This context applies to choices such as where to live, and who to spend the rest of your life with.

Drawing on this, I turn to the setting where menus consist of chance items, or gambles: both those where probabilities are given, such as '$100 if red comes up', typified by roulette; and those where probabilities are not given, such as 'Avocado if Pegasus wins the Derby', typified by racing. The discussion here applies to choices such as, in the first case, whether to undergo an operation if you are told that the mortality rate is 25 per cent, and, in the second, whether to travel by air in the face of terrorist threats.

As a digression, I then consider a special case of this setting, that where chance items involve only money. In this case attitudes to risk, as manifest in gambling and insurance, become relevant. This digression applies particularly to choices such as which form to hold your wealth in, and whether to insure your house.

Returning to the main story, I consider the case where menus consist of strategic items, such as making a high or a low auction bid, or, more generally, conflict or cooperation. The discussion here applies to choices such as when to travel if you know that everyone else is trying to avoid the rush-hour, and, for a nation, whether to develop a nuclear capability when others face the same choice.

The discussion thus far is that of individual choice. I conclude with a discussion of group choice, exploring mechanisms, such as democracy and dictatorship, for achieving this. This discussion applies to matters such as the choice of a restaurant by a group of friends and, on a larger scale, the relative advantages of 'first past the post' and proportional representation in elections. The connections between these settings are illustrated in the figure.

In the core discussion in each setting I proceed in four stages. First, I give some examples in which something seems amiss: an instance might be the Sandwich example discussed above. Second, I suggest what general problems might lie behind these examples: in the Sandwich example I suggest that what is wrong is that your choice changes when the menu is enlarged by the addition of something which you do not want. Third, I propose as a condition for rational choice that such problems should not arise; this in effect defines what it means to be rational. In the Sandwich example the condition might be that the addition to the menu of some irrelevant item should not affect your choice; and choice would then be

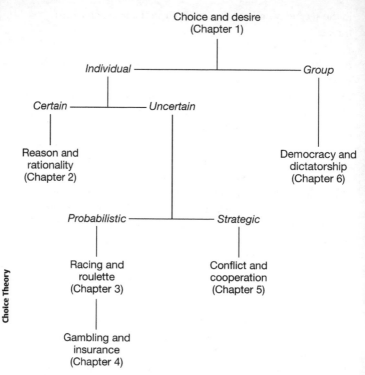

Choice and desire
(Chapter 1)

Individual — Group

Certain — Uncertain

Reason and
rationality
(Chapter 2)

Democracy and
dictatorship
(Chapter 6)

Probabilistic — Strategic

Racing and
roulette
(Chapter 3)

Conflict and
cooperation
(Chapter 5)

Gambling and
insurance
(Chapter 4)

Choice Theory

3. A family tree of choice theory

considered to be rational if it satisfied this condition. (In fact, as we shall see, this condition, although necessary, is not sufficient for choice to be considered rational.) Fourth, I find a procedure for achieving choice which is rational in this sense; that is, I provide a characterization of rational choice. In the Sandwich context the characterization might be that your choice is rational if and only if you can list all the items in some order and choose those at the top of your list. A summary of the discussion of these four stages is given at the end of the relevant chapter; as well as repeating the main points, this provides, in addition to the glossary, a convenient place in which to refer to various definitions.

Having dealt with the core ideas in each setting I look, more briefly, at some extensions. I start by making some observations on how, if at all, the story changes if time enters the picture in an essential way.

I then present (what is claimed to be) an empirical paradox. This is typically an instance where people taking part in laboratory experiments appear to act irrationally. There are a number of possible responses to such paradoxes. First, we can presume that people act differently when faced with real, or significant, choices than when faced with artificial, or insignificant, ones: you may take more care if what is at risk is your house rather than a mere $10 reward. Second, we can accept that we all make mistakes from time to time: the fact that you negligently make an irrational choice does not imply that you would keep to it if its irrationality were pointed out to you. Third, we may interpret choice theory as an exploration of what it means to be rational and, possibly, as a guide to making sensible decisions, rather than as a description of how people act in practice. Fourth, we can attempt to revise the theory to take account of the paradox. However, revising the theory to resolve one particular paradox may well create more problems than it solves: the maxim 'hard cases make bad law' should be borne in mind. You should formulate your own response to each of these paradoxes.

I conclude, as an application of choice theory, with a discussion of whether this theory throws any light on what might be meant by a just distribution of wealth, that is, on what is known as *distributive justice*. Indeed, the implications of choice theory for distributive justice may be considered a subplot of the main story.

As I have noted, we may interpret choice theory either as an exploration of what it means to be rational or as a description of how people act in practice. If we adopt the latter interpretation we should not confuse 'a description' with 'an explanation'. The claim would be not that people deliberately carry out the various calculations which the theory might suggest, just that, on the whole,

9

they act as if they do. A good description of the way in which a tree grows is obtained by assuming that it develops leaves in a way which maximizes the area exposed to the sun. But not even a tree-hugger would seriously suggest that the tree does this deliberately.

If we interpret choice theory as an exploration of what it means to be rational then the theory may also serve as a guide to making sensible decisions. But it will not, for example, suggest that you should gamble or that you should insure, for individual choices cannot be reasonable or unreasonable. (It might, however, suggest that you would be unwise to do both.) Similarly, it cannot advise Renton to choose, or not choose, life. In fact, he does eventually choose life, though without any marked enthusiasm:

> I'm moving on, going straight and choosing life. I'm looking forward to it already. I'm going to be just like you: the job, the family, the big television, the washing machine, the car, the compact disc and electrical tin opener, good health, low cholesterol, dental insurance, mortgage, starter home, leisurewear, luggage, three-piece suite . . . getting by, looking ahead, to the day you die.

Summary

Choice involves selecting one or more items from a menu. It is explored in four contexts: that of certainty, where all items are definite; that of uncertainty, where items involve chance, either with or without given probabilities; that of strategy, where two persons' individual choices are interdependent; and that of group choice, where a number of people must choose collectively. Attitudes to risk arise in the context of uncertainty and have implications in the context of strategy.

Chapter 2
Reason and rationality

The simplest framework for choice is that in which menus consist of
definite items, such as Avocado and $100, from which you must
choose one or more: ties are allowed. Recall that to say that two
items tie, that is, that you choose both jointly, is just to say that
you are equally content with either.

Reasonable choices

Consider the following example of apparently odd choices.

Hors d'œuvres example

Your menu consists of Asparagus, Beetroot, and Chicory: you
choose Asparagus. On your waiter, perhaps having misheard you,
telling you that Chicory is off you choose Beetroot. Your choices can
be represented schematically, using an obvious convention, as

ABC   *A*
AB   *B*

The problem with your choices in this example (which is, in essence,
the Sandwich example of Chapter 1) is that you choose *A* from the
full menu but do not choose *A* from *A* and *B*. This does not seem
right. To avoid such problems we might require that if you choose
some item from a menu and this item remains available in a more

restricted menu then you also choose it from the restricted menu. This requirement is the *contraction condition*; it is also known as Sen's alpha property, after Amartya Sen (born 1933), the Nobel prize-winning economist and philosopher. A racing analogy might be that if a filly wins a race which is open to both colts and fillies then she should also win if the race is restricted to fillies.

The contraction condition has an obvious implication. Assume that there are some ties in your original choice, and that you then choose again from the smaller menu consisting of all the tied items. As is easy to see, the contraction condition tells us that your choice does not change. This supports our allowing ties: if two items tie then there can be no reason for choosing one rather than the other.

A different type of problem arises in the next example.

Soup example

Choice Theory

Your menu seems to consist of Bean and Carrot soups: you choose Carrot. On your waiter telling you that you have misread Bean for Artichoke, so that in fact the menu consists of Artichoke and Carrot soups, you choose both jointly, that is, they tie. On your waiter returning to announce that Bean soup is indeed available, as well as the other two, you choose Artichoke. Schematically,

$$ABC \quad A$$
$$BC \quad C$$
$$AC \quad AC$$

The problem with your choices in this example is that you choose C from B and C and also, although not uniquely, from A and C, but do not choose C from the full menu. Again, this does not seem right. I shall say that you choose one item in a *pairwise* choice with a second if you choose the first, not necessarily alone, when your menu consists of just these two items. Now to avoid the type of problem encountered in the Soup example we might require that if you choose some item in pairwise choices with every other item on the menu then you choose it, though not necessarily it alone, from the full menu. This requirement is the *expansion condition*; it is also known as the Condorcet condition, after the Marquis Marie Jean Antoine Nicolas Caritat de Condorcet (1743–94), a mathematician and leading light of the French Enlightenment. A racing analogy here might be that if a filly beats each of a number of other fillies in two-horse races then she should also win a race whose field consists of her and these other fillies.

We should check that these two conditions are consistent, in that they both can be satisfied simultaneously, and independent, in that neither implies the other. The simplest way to do this is give an example which satisfies both conditions, an example which satisfies only the first, and an example which satisfies only the second. To show that an example fails to satisfy a condition we need only find one instance where it fails. However, to show that it satisfies a condition we must show that the condition is satisfied in all instances, that is, by choices from all possible menus.

Here is an example which satisfies both conditions (even though, as we shall see, the choices made in it still leave something to be desired).

Fish example

Your menu consists of Anchovies, Bass, and Cod: you choose Anchovies. But if your menu is restricted to Anchovies and Bass you choose both; if to Bass and Cod you choose Cod; and if to Anchovies and Cod you choose Anchovies. Schematically,

ABC A
AB AB
BC C
AC A

Note that this example specifies the choices which you make from all possible (non-trivial) menus. Here you choose A, the only item which you choose from the full menu, from any restricted menu in which it is available so that the contraction condition is satisfied. Also, *A* is the only item which you choose in pairwise choices with every other item so that the expansion condition is satisfied.

We can use the Soup example to provide an instance where the contraction but not the expansion condition is satisfied, provided that we complete this example by specifying that you choose *A* from *A* and *B*. Your choices are then

ABC	A
AB	A
BC	C
AC	AC

Now you choose *A*, the only item which you choose from the full menu, from any restricted menu in which it is available so that the contraction condition is satisfied. But, which is the point of the Soup example, the expansion condition fails: you choose *C*, albeit not uniquely, in pairwise choices with each other item but do not choose *C* from the full menu.

Similarly, we can use the Hors d'œuvres example to provide an instance where the expansion condition but not the contraction condition is satisfied, provided that we complete this example by specifying that you choose *C* from *B* and *C*, and that you choose *A* from *A* and *C*. Your choices are then

ABC	A
AB	B
BC	C
AC	A

Now you choose no item in pairwise choices with every other item so that, by default, the expansion condition is satisfied. (Recall that the expansion condition requires that if you choose some item in pairwise choices with every other item on the menu then you choose it from the full menu: if there is no item which you choose in all pairwise choices then the condition is satisfied automatically.) But, which is the point of this example, the contraction condition fails: you choose *A* from the full menu but do not choose *A* from *A* and *B*.

The Hors d'œuvres, Soup, and Fish examples show that the contraction and the expansion conditions are consistent and independent. As these conditions at least rule out the problems which I have identified so far I shall say that a *reasonable* choice process is one which satisfies these conditions. (Note that, for motives which will become apparent, I am using the term 'reasonable' rather than 'rational'.)

In order to characterize reasonable choices we need the concept of a *preference relation*. This specifies, for any two items on a menu, whether the first is at least as good as the second, or the second is at least as good as the first. This allows for the possibility of both applying: if this is the case then the two items are said to be indifferent. And if the first is at least as good as the second but the two are not indifferent then the first is said to be better than the second. This 'at least as good as' relation applies to menu items. An analogous relation which applies to people is the 'at least as tall as' relation: I am at least as tall as you; or you are at least as tall as me; or both, in which case we are of the same height.

Your choice is *explained by a preference relation* if, for some 'at least as good as' relation, the items which you choose from a menu are precisely those which are at least as good as every other item on the menu. This means that both (*a*) if an item is at least as good as every other item then you choose that item, and (*b*) if anything is better than an item then you do not choose that item. If your choice is explained by some preference relation it is easy to say what this relation is: it is the relation which specifies that one item is at least as good as a second if and only if you choose it, not necessarily

15

alone, from the pair. Note that this implies that if you choose an item alone from a pair then it is better than the other item.

Return to the Fish example, your choices in which are

ABC	*A*
AB	*AB*
BC	*C*
AC	*A*

By looking at the three pairwise choices it is clear that, if your preference relation was

A is indifferent to *B*
C is better than *B*
A is better than *C*

and you always chose the best available items, then you would have chosen exactly as you did, in fact, choose in that example. This is to say that your choice would have been explained by a preference relation.

It might seem that all choices can be explained by some preference relation, however bizarre. This is not the case. Return to the Hors d'œuvres example, your choices in which are

ABC	*A*
AB	*B*

If these choices could be explained by a preference relation then *A* would have to be at least as good as *B* because you choose *A* from the full menu; and *B* would have to be better than *A* because you choose *B* alone from *A* and *B*. As both of these cannot be true there can be no preference relation which explains your choices.

The same conclusion applies in the Soup example, your choices in which are

ABC   A
BC   C
AC   AC

Here either *A* or *B* would have to be better than *C* as you do not choose *C* from the full menu; but *A* is not better than *C* as you choose *C*, even though not alone, from *A* and *C*; and *B* is not better than *C* as you choose *C* from *B* and *C*. Thus, again, there can be no preference relation which explains your choices.

The Hors d'œuvres and Soup examples suggest that (*a*) choices cannot be explained by a preference relation if either the contraction or the expansion condition (or both) fails, that is, if choices are not reasonable, and (*b*) choices can be explained by a preference relation if both conditions hold, that is, if choices are reasonable. This indeed is the case: choice is reasonable if and only if it can be explained by a preference relation.

This means that, if choice is reasonable, choices and preference relations are effectively the same: we can always derive choices from preference relations; and we can always derive preference relations from choices.

Rational choices

Reasonableness is a good starting point, but there may be more to be said, as I suggested when introducing the Fish example, your choices in which are

ABC   A
AB   AB
BC   C
AC   A

The problem here is that in one instance you choose B when A is available, while in another you choose A when B is available without also choosing B. We may interpret this as meaning that in the first instance B is revealed as being at least as good as A, while in the second A is revealed as being better than B. To avoid such problems we might require that if you ever choose one item when a second item is available then whenever you choose the second and the first is available you also choose the first. This requirement is the *revelation condition*; it is also known as Samuelson's revealed preference condition, after Paul Samuelson (born 1915), another Nobel prize-winning economist. A racing analogy here might be that, if one filly wins, either outright or in a dead-heat, a race in which a second filly runs then the second will not win outright any race in which the first runs.

It is easy to see that the revelation condition implies both the contraction condition and the expansion condition. However, in the Fish example, for instance, the revelation condition fails, as we have seen, but the contraction and expansion conditions hold. Thus the revelation condition is stronger than the contraction and expansion conditions together. That is, any choices which satisfy the revelation condition satisfy the contraction and expansion conditions, but choices can satisfy the contraction and expansion conditions without satisfying the revelation condition.

The revelation condition has some bite: choices in the Fish example do not satisfy it. But it does not have too much bite: it can be satisfied, as the following example shows.

Meat example

Your menu consists of Alligator, Beef, Chicken, and Duck. If Alligator is available you choose it; failing that you choose Beef if it is available; failing that you choose Chicken and Duck jointly. Schematically,

ABCD	A	AC	A
ABC	A	AD	A
ABD	A	BC	B
ACD	A	BD	B
BCD	B	CD	CD
AB	A		

It is easy to see that your choices in this example satisfy the revelation condition. This implies that they also satisfy the contraction and expansion conditions and thus are reasonable. Accordingly, they can be represented by a preference relation, which is

A is better than *B*	*B* is better than *C*
A is better than *C*	*B* is better than *D*
A is better than *D*	*C* is indifferent to *D*

As the revelation condition at least rules out the problems with reasonable choices which I have identified I shall say that a *rational choice* process is one which satisfies this condition.

To characterize rational choice we need the concept of a *preference ordering*. This is a particular type of preference relation, one which is what is known as *transitive*. An 'at least as good as' relation is transitive if, when *X* is at least as good as *Y*, and *Y* is at least as good as *Z*, then *X* is at least as good as *Z*. For example, the 'at least as tall as' relation among people is transitive: if I am at least as tall as you, and you are at least as tall as Montmorency, then I am at least as tall as Montmorency. The preference relation underlying the Meat example is transitive, and thus a preference ordering. Even though transitivity seems a natural property of a preference relation not all preference relations are transitive: for instance, the preference relation underlying the Fish example, which is

A is indifferent to *B*
C is better than *B*
A is better than *C*

is not transitive: if it were the first two statements would imply that
C is at least as good as A, which would contradict the last.

A preference ordering is so called because it allows items to be
ordered, albeit with ties. This means that we can arrange all the
items in a list, with the best at the top and the worst at the bottom.
Return to the preference ordering underlying the Meat example.
Using an obvious convention the list is

A
B
CD

We could not arrange items in a list without transitivity. If, for the
preference relation underlying the Fish example, we put A at the
top of the list then we must put B at the top as well because A is
indifferent to B; but we cannot put B at the top because C is
better than B; and we cannot put C at the top because A is better
than C. Thus we can put no item at the top so we cannot make a
list.

Your choice is *explained by a preference ordering* if it is explained by
a preference relation which is transitive. (Recall that a preference
ordering is just a transitive preference relation.) As we have seen,
the preference relation underlying the choices made in the Fish
example, for which the revelation condition fails, is not transitive so
that these choices cannot be explained by a preference ordering. On
the other hand, the choices made in the Meat example, for which
this condition holds, can.

The Meat and Fish examples suggest that (*a*) choices cannot be
explained by a preference ordering if the revelation condition fails,
that is, if choices are not rational, and (*b*) choices can be explained
by a preference ordering if this condition holds, that is, if choices
are rational. This indeed is the case: choice is rational if and only if
it can be explained by a preference ordering.

4. *The Thinker*: choice is deliberate desire (Auguste Rodin, 1904)

This means that, if choice is rational, choices and preference orderings are effectively the same. Indeed, we can consider the preference ordering underlying choice as the reason for that choice: there is an intimate connection between reason and rationality: 'choice is deliberate desire'.

Utility

Just as rational choices can be represented by preference orderings, preference orderings can in turn be represented by utilities. A utility representation for an 'at least as good as' ordering assigns numbers to items in such a way that better items have higher numbers. More precisely, one item has a greater *utility* than a second if and only if the first is better than the second. For the preference ordering underlying the Meat example, which is

A is better than B   B is better than C
A is better than C   B is better than D
A is better than D   C is indifferent to D

we can assign the utilities

A	3
B	2
C	1
D	1

This assignment is instructive. It suggests that we can always assign utilities for a preference ordering by making a list, assigning the number 1 to the bottom item (or items), 2 to the next, and so on until we reach the top. Indeed, this is obviously the case: we can always represent a preference ordering by utilities. This argument also makes it clear that we cannot represent a preference relation which is not a preference ordering, that is, which is not transitive, by utilities, for in this case we cannot make a list.

There are many other ways to assign utilities. An alternative way of assigning utilities in the present case is

A	100
B	99
C	10
D	10

Neither of these ways is better than the other. They both mean one thing and one thing only: that A is better than everything else; B is better than C and D; and C and D are indifferent. For this reason utility in the sense used here is known as *ordinal utility*: all it does is order things. Ordinal utilities can be transformed in any increasing way, for example (provided they are positive), by squaring or taking square roots, without affecting their representational property.

Your choice is *utility maximizing* if, for some assignment of utilities, the items which you choose are precisely those whose utility is at least as great as that of every other item. If this is the case then choice maximizes utility. Clearly this can only be the case if choices can be represented by a preference ordering, for if there is no preference ordering there can be no utility assignment; and if choices are represented by a preference ordering then they must maximize utility. In other words, choice is utility maximizing if and only if it can be explained by a preference ordering. Then since choice is rational if and only if it can be explained by a preference ordering we can say that choice is rational if and only if it is utility maximizing.

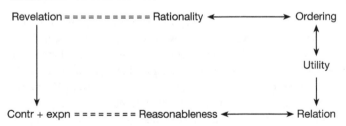

5. **A map of choice under certainty: equality signs represent definitions, double arrows represent equivalence, and single arrows represent implications**

In a formal sense, then, choosing rationally is the same as maximizing utility. But the interpretation is vital. You prefer X to Y if you choose X alone from X and Y, and you assign a greater utility to X than to Y if you prefer X to Y. Utility is derived from choice, not choice from utility. You do not choose to go riding rather than skiing because it gives you more utility; on the contrary, a greater utility is assigned to riding because you choose it.

The connections between reasonableness, rationality and the various conditions proposed in this chapter are illustrated in the figure.

Some extensions

The picture changes little if time becomes relevant. Many choices involving time do not involve it in any essential way. Consider, for example, choosing today what to consume today and tomorrow. Although this choice involves time it immediately fits into a timeless framework. The only difference is that, instead choosing from the two items X and Y, say, you choose from the four items

X today and X tomorrow
X today and Y tomorrow
Y today and X tomorrow
Y today and Y tomorrow

However, not all choices fit this pattern. Someone, if not Renton, may avoid heroin because he knows that if he has some today he will be its slave tomorrow. More generally, it may be that today you want 'X today and Y tomorrow' but you know that if you have X today then your preferences will change so that you will want X tomorrow as well. This is, in essence, the problem faced by Homer's (c.700 BCE) hero Ulysses, who has himself tied to the mast of his ship so that he can hear the sirens' sweet song without, later, being driven to follow the seductive sound and perish. The timeless theory developed here cannot deal with problems of this type.

Even in a timeless framework all may not be straightforward. Consider an apparent paradox, known as the framing paradox. You are in a shop, having decided to buy a telephone for $20 and a computer for $1000. First, you are told that the telephone is $10 cheaper at another branch, some five minutes walk away: do you buy now or go to the other branch? Second, you are told that the computer (but not the telephone) is $10 cheaper at the other branch: do you buy now or go to the other branch? Pause and consider.

Clearly you should make the same choice in each case as the two problems are the same in substance, differing only in spin, or framing: in each case you save $10 by going to the other branch. But significantly more people questioned in an experiment chose to go to the other branch when the telephone was reduced than did when the computer was reduced. I noted various possible responses to paradoxes such as this in Chapter 1. You should formulate your own response to this one.

An important implication of the fact that utilities can be transformed in any increasing way without affecting their representational property is that comparisons of changes in utility have no meaning. Consider, for example, the claim that the difference between the utility of $1000 and that of $2000 is greater than the difference between the utility of $8000 and that of $9000. This is equivalent to the claim that $1000 gives more utility when added to $1000 than it does when added to $8000, or that the *marginal utility* of $1000 is greater when you are poor than when you are rich. Claims such as this are neither true nor false: they are meaningless.

Assuming that more wealth is preferred to less, one way of allocating utilities is to assign to each sum of money (expressed in thousands of dollars) a utility equal to that sum; a second way is to assign a utility equal to the square root of that sum; and a third way is to assign a utility equal to the square of that sum. Each way is, of course, equally good.

Then the claim that the difference between the utility of $1000 and that of $2000 is greater than the difference between the utility of $8000 and that of $9000 appears true if utility is assigned in the square root way, where the two marginal utilities are approximately 0.4 and 0.2 respectively; and it appears false if utility is assigned in the square way, where the two figures are 17 and 3. But each of these ways of assigning utilities is equally good: neither of the calculations means anything.

Beliefs such as this arise from a confusion between the correct statement 'greater utility is assigned to more wealth because more wealth is preferred' with the meaningless statement 'more wealth is preferred because it gives greater utility'. A misguided application of such thinking calls for the redistribution of wealth, for example by progressive taxation, on the grounds that a poor person gains 'more' from receiving $1000 than a rich one loses by paying $1000. Again, this is meaningless. And in this case the confusion is compounded by an unjustifiable attempt to compare different people's utilities. There is no reason why we should not adopt, say, the square root way of assigning utilities for everyone. But if we do this then the fact that your utility level is twice mine tells us precisely what we already know, that your wealth is four times mine, and nothing more. Utility is not a measure of happiness or well-being: it is simply a numerical representation of preference.

Summary

Choice under certainty involves choosing one or more definite items from a given menu.

The contraction condition requires that if you choose some item from a menu and this item remains available in a more restricted menu then you also choose it from the restricted menu.

The expansion condition requires that if you choose some item in pairwise choices with every other item on the menu then you choose it, though not necessarily it alone, from the full menu.

Choice is explained by a preference relation if, for some 'at least as good as' relation, the items which you choose are precisely those which are at least as good as every other item on the menu.

Choice is reasonable, that is, satisfies the contraction and expansion conditions, if and only if it can be explained by a preference relation.

The revelation condition requires that if you ever choose one item when a second item is available then whenever you choose the second and the first is available you also choose the first.

Choice is explained by a preference ordering if it is explained by a preference relation which is transitive.

Choice is rational, that is, satisfies the revelation condition, if and only if it is explained by a preference ordering.

A utility representation for an 'at least as good as' ordering assigns numbers to items in such a way that one item has a greater utility number than a second if and only if the first is better than the second; your choice is utility maximizing if, for some assignment of utilities, the items which you choose are precisely those whose utility is at least as great as that of every other item.

Choice is rational if and only if it is utility maximizing.

Chapter 3
Racing and roulette

I now turn to the case where menus consist of chance items such as '$100 if red comes up' and 'Avocado if Pegasus wins the Derby'. In the first case, typified by roulette, probabilities are given; in the second case, typified by racing, they must be inferred.

The setting

The *probability* of an outcome is a number, in the range 0 to 1, which quantifies how likely the outcome is: the higher the probability the more likely the outcome. At the extremes, a probability of 0 implies impossibility and a probability of 1 implies certainty. Probabilities have three basic properties. First, the probabilities of all possible outcomes add up to 1. Thus if all slots on a 36-slot roulette wheel are equally likely then the probability of any given number coming up is 1/36. Second, if two outcomes cannot both occur together then the probability of either of them occurring is the sum of the probabilities of each occurring. Thus the probability of a 7 or a 12 coming up is 2/36, and, using this property repeatedly, the probability of an even number coming up is 18/36, or 0.5. Third, the probability of two independent outcomes occurring consecutively is the product of the probabilities of their each occurring. Thus the probability of even numbers coming up twice in a row is 0.5 × 0.5, or 0.25.

Menu items under uncertainty are called gambles. A *probability gamble* is a list of possible prizes with a probability attached to each; clearly, these probabilities must add up to 1. An example is '$100 with probability 0.5 and nothing with probability 0.5', or, equivalently, '$100 with probability 0.5 and nothing otherwise'. Another example is 'nothing with probability 0.5, Bacon with probability 0.25, and Cheese otherwise'. We may write these two gambles, say X and Y, as

$100 wp 0.5 and nothing wp 0.5

and

Nothing wp 0.5, Bacon wp 0.25, and Cheese otherwise

respectively, where 'wp' stands for 'with probability'.

You may imagine that the outcomes of gambles are determined by someone behind the scenes spinning a roulette wheel. If you have chosen gamble X and an even number comes up you receive $100 and if an odd number comes up you receive nothing. If you have chosen gamble Y and a number in the range 1 to 18 comes up you receive Avocado, if a number in the range 19 to 27 comes up you receive Bacon, and if a number in the range 28 to 36 comes up you receive Cheese.

It will be convenient to consider 'Avocado with probability 1', which would more naturally be called simply Avocado, to be a gamble; this is said to be a *degenerate gamble*. Also, the prizes of a gamble may themselves be gambles. An example of such a gamble, the prizes of which are the gamble X and the gamble Y, is

Gamble X wp 0.6 and gamble Y wp 0.4

This *compound gamble* may be seen as a *mixture* of the two component gambles X and Y with the weights 0.6 and 0.4

29

respectively. Such a mixture is a gamble whose prizes are all the prizes of X and Y; the probabilities associated with the prizes of X are their original probabilities multiplied by 0.6, and the probabilities associated with the prizes of Y are their original probabilities multiplied by 0.4. Thus, for example, the probability associated with \$100, which is a prize of X, is 0.6×0.5, or 0.3; and that associated with nothing, which is a prize of both X and Y, is $(0.6 \times 0.5) + (0.4 \times 0.5)$, or 0.5. This compound gamble, or mixture, is equivalent to the simple gamble

\$100 wp 0.3, nothing wp 0.5, Bacon wp 0.1, and Cheese wp 0.1

as is illustrated in the figure.

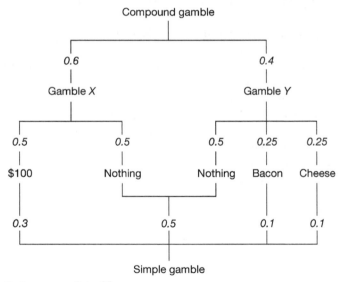

6. A compound gamble

With these preliminaries out of the way we can turn our attention to choice from gambles. We can immediately draw on the discussion of Chapter 2: merely changing the name of a menu item from

Asparagus to '$100 with probability 0.5 and nothing otherwise' cannot change any of the results of that chapter. None the less, there may be more to matters here. For example, if you prefer $100 to nothing then it would seem natural that you would prefer the gamble which gives you $100 with probability 0.9 and nothing otherwise to the gamble which gives you $100 with probability 0.1 and nothing otherwise. However, the concept of rationality developed in Chapter 2 would not imply this: as far as that conception goes, this would be analogous to requiring that you prefer Chicken to Duck just because you prefer Alligator to Beef.

The reason why there may be more to matters here is that menu items under certainty have no internal structure: Avocado is simply Avocado. Menu items under uncertainty, on the other hand, have some internal structure: they involve both prizes and probabilities. This means that preference orderings under certainty are the end of the matter: they cannot be rational or irrational. But we can sensibly ask whether preference orderings under uncertainty are rational. For example, we can look at patterns in preferences over gambles with the same prizes but different probabilities, such as those involving $100 or nothing.

Probability gambles

In the light of this discussion I shall assume that choices from gambles can be explained by a preference ordering and ask what it means for this ordering to be rational. As I shall not be concerned with preference relations which are not orderings, that is, which are not transitive, I shall, from now on, refer to preference orderings simply as *preferences*.

Consider the following example in which something seems amiss.

Vegetables example

You prefer Aubergine to Broccoli but, knowing that the service is haphazard and that whichever you ask for you have a 0.1 probability of getting Cauliflowers, you ask for Broccoli: that is, you prefer 'Broccoli with probability 0.9 and Cauliflowers otherwise' to 'Aubergine with probability 0.9 and Cauliflowers otherwise'.

The problem with your choices in this example is that in the second instance the outcome C is the same for each gamble yet you let it influence you. It would seem more natural if, when comparing two gambles, you were to ignore the aspects in which they were the same and concentrate on the ones in which they differ. Of course, you might prefer '0.9 of a B and 0.1 of a C' to '0.9 of an A and 0.1 of a C' even though you prefer A alone to B alone (perhaps because C goes better with B than it does with A). However, neither of these is being offered. Either you will get what you have ordered, or you will get C. If you get what you have ordered then C is irrelevant; if you get C then it does not matter what you have ordered. To ensure that such irrelevancies do not cloud the picture we might require that if you prefer one gamble to a second then you prefer any mixture of the first gamble and some third gamble to a mixture of the second gamble and the third with the same weights. This requirement is the *substitution condition*.

The substitution condition has an immediate implication. This is that if you prefer \$100 to nothing then you prefer the gamble which gives you \$100 with probability 0.9 and nothing otherwise to the gamble which gives you \$100 with probability 0.1 and nothing otherwise. More generally, if you prefer one gamble to another then you prefer a mixture of the two to a second mixture if and only if the weight of the better gamble in the first mixture is greater than that in the second.

A different type of problem arises in the next example.

Fruit example

You prefer Apples to Bananas and Bananas to Cherries (and, being rational, Apples to Cherries). However, you prefer Bananas to every gamble which gives you either Apples or the detested Cherries, however low the probability of getting the latter.

The problem with your choices in this example is that there is a jump in your preference. Consider your preference between B and the gamble X which gives you A with probability p and C otherwise for some probability p. If p is less than 1, however close to 1 it may be, you prefer B; but when p is equal to 1, which is to say when the gamble X becomes simply A, you prefer X. Thus at some point you switch from preferring one to the other without passing through the intervening stage of being indifferent between the two. This is illustrated in the table.

p	0.9	0.99	0.999	...	1.0
Choice	B	B	B	...	X

It would seem more acceptable for your preference to change smoothly rather than jump like this. To see what this implies in practice reinterpret A as being \$1m, B as being nothing, and C as being your death. The claim is that for some sufficiently high probability p you would take the gamble which gives you \$1m with the probability p and results in your death otherwise. If this seems unlikely ask yourself whether you would cross a busy street, thus incurring a minute probability of death, to collect \$1m. Typically, the answer would be yes. To exclude jumps in preference we might require that if you prefer one gamble to a second and the second to a third then there is some mixture of the first and third which you consider indifferent to the second. This requirement is the *continuity condition*; it is also known as the Archimedean condition, after the Greek mathematician Archimedes (287–212 BCE).

(We might note parenthetically that the continuity condition requires that probabilities be allowed to vary continuously, for if they only varied in steps of 0.1, say, then it might well be that you preferred the gamble which gives you A with probability 0.9 and C otherwise to B, and preferred B to the gamble which gives you A

with probability 0.8 and *C* otherwise; this in turn requires there to be infinitely many possible gambles.)

We should again check that our two conditions are consistent and independent. To avoid repetition I shall only consider consistency; it is straightforward to check independence. Consistency is shown by the following example.

Nuts example

In contemplating all possible gambles involving Almonds, Brazils, and Cashews you prefer one gamble to a second whenever twice the probability of getting Almonds plus the probability of getting Brazils in the first gamble is greater than the corresponding number in the second.

In this example you prefer the gamble

A wp *p*, *B* wp *q*, and *C* otherwise

to the gamble

A wp *r*, *B* wp *s*, and *C* otherwise

whenever $2p + q$ is greater than $2r + s$. Note that this specifies your preferences between all possible gambles involving *A*, *B* and *C*. It is easy to show that the substitution and continuity conditions are satisfied.

As the substitution and continuity conditions are consistent and independent and seem at least to rule out the problems which I have identified, I shall say that you have *rational preferences* over gambles if your preferences satisfy these conditions.

To characterize rationality we need the concept of *expected utility*. Recall that we have assumed that choice from gambles can be explained by a preference ordering, or, equivalently, is utility maximizing (as discussed in Chapter 2). Then, as we can assign utilities to all gambles we can certainly assign them to degenerate gambles, that is, to prizes. Assume that we have done this. Then the expected utility of a gamble is obtained by multiplying the utility of each prize by the probability associated with that prize and adding the resulting numbers. For example, if you have the utility assignment

X	1
Y	3
Z	2

then the expected utility of the gamble

X wp 0.2, Y wp 0.3, and Z wp 0.5

is $(1 \times 0.2) + (3 \times 0.3) + (2 \times 0.5)$, or 2.1.

Recall that we can assign utilities in many ways: all that is required is that better prizes have higher utilities. For future reference note that if we double all utilities then we double the expected utility of any gamble, and if we add 7 to all utilities then we add 7 to the expected utility of any gamble. For example, if we do both of these, in that order, the new expected utility of the above gamble is 11.2, which is double the old expected utility plus 7. However, if we replace all utilities with their squares then the new expected utility is not the square of the old expected utility: the new expected utility is 4.9 but the square of the old expected utility is 4.41.

It would be convenient if we could assign utilities to prizes in such a way that we could judge gambles simply on the basis of their expected utilities, that is, in such a way that you prefer one gamble to a second if and only if it has a higher expected utility. This would mean, for example, that you would prefer the above gamble to the new gamble

X wp 0.5, Y wp 0.3, and Z wp 0.2

because the expected utility of the original gamble, which, as we have noted, is 2.1, exceeds that of the new one, which is 1.8. If it is possible to assign utilities in this way then the utilities so assigned are called *cardinal utilities*, or Bernoulli utilities, after the mathematician Daniel Bernoulli (1700–82), and preferences are said to have the *expected utility property*.

If we can assign cardinal utilities at all then we can assign them in many ways. Suppose that we have assigned cardinal utilities to prizes in one way. Then a gamble X is better than a gamble Y if and only if it has a higher expected utility under this assignment. Now we assign utilities to prizes in a different way, under which the new utility assigned to each prize is twice its old utility plus 7. As we have seen, this implies that the new expected utility of any gamble is twice its old expected utility plus 7. Then X has a higher new expected utility than Y if and only if it has a higher old expected utility, which is to say if and only if it is better than Y. Thus cardinal utilities retain their representational properties when they are doubled and have 7 added to them. More generally, they retain their representational properties when transformed in what is known as a *linear* way: that is, when they are multiplied (or divided) by any positive number or when any number is added to (or subtracted from) them. A familiar example of a linear transformation is that between two ways of measuring temperature: degrees Fahrenheit are simply degrees centigrade multiplied by 1.8 and then having 32 added.

On the other hand, cardinal utilities do not retain their representational properties when transformed in a non-linear way. This is because applying any other transformation to utilities does not result in expected utility being transformed in the same way. For example, if you have the utility assignment

X 5
Y 3
Z 0

then you prefer Y (that is, the degenerate gamble which gives you Y

with probability 1) to the gamble which gives you X with probability 0.5 and Z otherwise: the two expected utilities are 3 and 2.5. But if these utilities are replaced with their squares then the two expected utilities are 9 and 12.5, which would, wrongly, suggest that you prefer the gamble to Y.

Suppose that we have assigned cardinal utilities to prizes in such a way that a prize X has the utility v and a better prize Y has the utility u; obviously u must be greater than v. If we subtract v from these utilities and then divide the results by $u - v$ (which is positive) we have new cardinal utilities under which Y has the utility 1 and X has the utility 0. This means that if we can assign cardinal utilities at all then we can do this in a way which gives the utility 0 to one prize and 1 to some better prize.

The expected utility property applies in the Nuts example, in which you prefer one gamble to a second whenever twice the probability of getting A plus the probability of getting B in the first is greater than the corresponding number in the second. If we assign the utilities

A	2
B	1
C	0

then the expected utility of the gamble

A wp p, B wp q, and C otherwise

is $2p + q$; and that of the gamble

A wp r, B wp s, and C otherwise

is $2r + s$. Then as you prefer the first gamble to the second if and only if $2p + q$ is greater than $2r + s$ you prefer the first gamble to the second if and only if it has a higher expected utility. In other words, your preferences have the expected utility property.

To see that the expected utility property is not a trivial one return to the Vegetables example, in which you prefer A to B but also prefer the gamble X which gives you B with probability 0.9 and C otherwise to the gamble Y which gives you A with probability 0.9 and C otherwise. Since you prefer A to B we can assign a utility of 1 to A and 0 to B. Write the utility assigned to C as u. Then the expected utility of X is $0.1u$, and that of Y is $0.9 + 0.1u$. As you prefer X to Y the expected utility property would require $0.1u$ to be greater than $0.9 + 0.1u$, which is impossible.

A similar impasse awaits us in the Fruit example, in which you prefer A to B, and B to C, but prefer B to every gamble which gives either A or C. Since you prefer A to C we can assign a utility of 1 to A and 0 to C. Write the utility assigned to B as u. Then, as you prefer A to B, and B to C, u must lie between 0 and 1. Also, you prefer B to the gamble which gives you A with probability p and C otherwise for every probability p which is less than 1. Since the expected utility of the gamble is p, the expected utility property would require the fixed u of less than 1 to be greater than every possible such p. Again, this is impossible.

It is no coincidence that (a) the expected utility property holds in the Nuts but not in the Vegetables or Fruit examples, and (b) either the substitution or the continuity condition (or both) fails in the Vegetables and Fruit examples but both conditions are satisfied in the Nuts example. The expected utility property always holds whenever the two conditions are satisfied, which is to say whenever preferences are rational. We have then a complete characterization: preferences over (probability) gambles are rational if and only if they have the expected utility property.

Some extensions

The picture changes somewhat if time becomes relevant. Consider two gambles, each of which gives you $1m in one year's time (measured from today) if an even number comes up at roulette and nothing otherwise. The two gambles, however, are not identical: in the first gamble the roulette wheel is spun today, while in the second it is spun in one year's time. Not only are they not identical, but you would be unlikely to consider them to be identical. You would typically prefer the first because knowledge of your future wealth would enable you to plan your life over the next year more advantageously. If you knew that you were going to be rich then you might run down your savings, or borrow against your future $1m, in the coming year. However, the timeless theory developed here cannot distinguish between the two gambles and cannot, therefore, deal with choices where time enters the picture in this way.

Even in a timeless framework all may not be straightforward. Consider an apparent paradox, known as the Allais paradox, after Maurice Allais (born 1911), the Nobel prize-winning economist. First, do you prefer the (degenerate) gamble U which is

$240 wp 1

to the gamble V which is

$250 wp 0.33, $240 wp 0.66, and $0 wp 0.01?

Second, do you prefer the gamble X which is

$250 wp 0.33 and $0 wp 0.67

to the gamble Y which is

$240 wp 0.34 and $0 wp 0.66?

Pause and consider. If you prefer the gamble U to the gamble V then you should also prefer Y to X. To see why this is the case assign a utility of 1 to $250 and 0 to nothing, and write the utility assigned to $240 as u. Then if you prefer U to V the (expected) utility of U, which is u, must be greater than the expected utility of V, which is

39

$0.33 + 0.66u$. This implies that $0.34u$ must be greater than 0.33. Since $0.34u$ is the expected utility of Y and 0.33 is the expected utility of X this in turn implies that, if your preferences have the expected utility property, you prefer Y to X.

However, in an experiment a significant proportion of people claimed to prefer U to V and also to prefer X to Y. This means that the preferences of these people did not have the expected utility property, or, equivalently, did not satisfy either the substitution condition or the continuity condition (in fact, the former). The cause of this seems to be that people attach too much importance to outcomes with very small probabilities. (This may go some way to explaining why people buy tickets in national lotteries which offer immense prizes with minute probabilities.) Make what you will of this, bearing in mind the possible responses to paradoxes which I noted in Chapter 1.

An implication of the fact that cardinal utilities retain their representational properties when transformed in a linear way but not when transformed in a non-linear way is that differences in utility now have some meaning. If the difference between the utilities in one pair of prizes is greater than that in a second pair for one way of assigning cardinal utilities then it is greater for all ways. It seems, then, that cardinal utility may provide a basis for arguments in favour of the redistribution of wealth. This question is best addressed in the context where all prizes are sums of money; accordingly, I shall delay its discussion until the next chapter.

State gambles

So far, probabilities have been given. To discuss choice where probabilities are not given we need the concept of states of the world, or, more simply, states. A *state* is a specification of everything which is relevant to your choice and about which you are uncertain. In the context of a two-horse race (and assuming that at least one horse will finish and there is not a dead-heat) the states might be

7. Alcove not winning: Alcove, ridden by the author, is second from the left

'Alcove wins' and 'Barathea wins'. As this example suggests, states must be specified in such a way that one and only one will occur.

A *state gamble* is a list of possible prizes with, for each, a specification of the state in which it will be received. An example in the present context would be 'Gain $200 if Alcove wins and lose $100 if Barathea wins'. We may write this as

+ $200 if A and –$100 if B

If the odds for Alcove were 2 to 1 (stake $1 to win $2) we could with some sense call this gamble 'Bet $100 on Alcove'. If the odds for Barathea were 1 to 2 the gamble 'Bet $100 on Barathea' would be

$$- \$100 \text{ if } A \text{ and } + \$50 \text{ if } B$$

State gambles are analogous to probability gambles in that they each list a number of prizes with circumstances attached: the difference is that the circumstances are now states rather than probabilities. States allow us to think about choice from gambles when probabilities are not given. This is of some importance. In almost all interesting contexts probabilities are not given: you are not given the probability of Alcove winning, of your car being stolen, or of the stock market collapsing.

How might you sensibly choose from gambles when probabilities are not given? A plausible suggestion is that you would (*a*) assign subjective probabilities to states, then (*b*) assign utilities to prizes, and then (*c*) choose the gamble which gives you the highest *subjective expected utility* given these probabilities. To illustrate this procedure return to our race and consider choosing between the gambles 'Bet $100 on Alcove' and 'Bet $100 on Barathea'. You first assign probabilities to states: say 0.4 to Alcove winning and 0.6 to Barathea winning. You then assign utilities to prizes. There are three possible prizes:

+$200 (if you bet on *A* and he wins)
+$50   (if you bet on *B* and he wins)
−$100 (if your horse loses)

You then assign utilities to these prizes, say

+$200   5
+$50   3
−$100   0

Finally, you compute the expected utility of each gamble given these probabilities: 2 if you bet on Alcove and 1.8 if you bet on Barathea. As the subjective expected utility of betting on Alcove is greater than that of betting on Barathea you bet on Alcove. If you act in this way your preferences over gambles have the *subjective expected utility property*. The utilities which you assign are, of course, cardinal, and may be transformed in any linear way, though not in any other way.

To introduce some variety I shall in this context work backwards: that is, I shall start by assuming the subjective expected utility property and then see what conditions might support this. And, as the arguments are quite similar to those in the setting where probabilities are given, I shall not go into as much detail as in that setting.

The basic idea is beautifully simple. It is that by looking at patterns of choices you can unscramble utilities and probabilities. If you choose a gamble in which you receive Avocado if the sun shines and Cheese otherwise rather than one in which you receive Bacon if the sun shines and Cheese otherwise this suggests that you prefer Avocado to Bacon and thus assign it a higher utility. And if you also choose a gamble in which you receive Avocado if the sun shines and Bacon otherwise rather than one in which you receive Avocado if it is raining and Bacon otherwise this suggests that you consider sun more likely than rain and thus assign it a higher probability. By conducting sufficiently many such thought experiments you can assign utilities to all prizes and probabilities to all states. Having done so, you naturally act as if you had been given these utilities and probabilities and choose so as to maximize your expected utility.

If your preferences have the subjective expected utility property then both your tastes, represented by utilities, and your beliefs, represented by probabilities, are subjective. Also, your tastes and beliefs are independent: you do not value something more because

43

you think it more likely, or think it more likely because you value it more. Further, the utility which you assign to a prize does not depend on the state in which you receive it: $200 means the same to you whether Alcove wins or loses. This last requirement is quite strong. It might be acceptable in the case of a race but seems less so in other settings.

Consider, for example, speculating on the euro exchange rate, expressed as the price of a euro in dollars. To keep matters simple I shall assume that there are only two possible states: the rate rises, and the rate falls. You have two possible gambles: buy euros, and sell euros. If you buy and the rate moves up you gain $100 but if it falls you lose $100; if you sell and the rate moves up you lose $100 but if it falls you gain $100. The complication is that gaining $100 when the exchange rate has risen is not the same as gaining $100 when the exchange rate has fallen: the cost of any imported items which you buy will be higher in the first case than it is in the second. More generally, the utility which you assign to a prize depends on the state in which it is received.

If, in the light of this example, it is felt that the subjective expected utility property is too demanding we could be less ambitious and allow utilities to depend on states. For example, instead of assigning utilities of, say, 0 to losing $100 and 1 to gaining $100 you might assign the utilities

Gain $100 in fall state	4
Gain $100 in rise state	3
Lose $100 in fall state	1
Lose $100 in rise state	0

Multiplying such utilities by the relevant probabilities and adding the resulting numbers gives the *state-dependent subjective expected utility* of a gamble. If you choose the gamble with the highest state-dependent subjective expected utility your preferences are said to have the *state-dependent subjective expected utility property*.

Clearly, this is a weaker property than the (full) subjective expected utility property.

To see what conditions might support the (full or state-dependent) subjective expected utility property we must explicitly allow the prizes of state gambles themselves to be gambles, just as we allowed the prizes of probability gambles to be gambles. We can then interpret mixtures of state gambles in a way directly analogous to mixtures of probability gambles. This in turn allows us to apply the substitution and continuity conditions to state gambles: recall that each of these conditions is expressed in terms of mixtures only, and does not mention probabilities.

Once we have done this we can immediately characterize the state-dependent subjective expected utility property. Preferences have this property if and only if they satisfy the substitution and continuity conditions (as applied to state gambles).

The substitution and continuity conditions do not, however, ensure that preferences have the full subjective expected utility property. This requires a further condition: that if you prefer one gamble to another in one state then you prefer it in all states. This condition, known as the *impartiality condition*, is much more restrictive than the other conditions we have encountered. Suppose that the two states are rain and sun, and one (degenerate) gamble gives an umbrella with certainty and another gives a bottle of water with certainty. Then you might well, in contravention of the impartiality condition, prefer the umbrella in the rain state and the water in the sun state.

Restrictive though it may be, the impartiality condition, together with the other two conditions, gives us the characterization we seek. Preferences have the full subjective expected utility property if and only if they satisfy the substitution and continuity conditions (as applied to state gambles) and the impartiality condition.

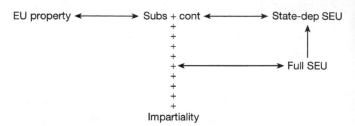

8. A map of choice under uncertainty: (S)EU stands for (subjective) expected utility, plus signs represent combinations, double arrows represent equivalence, and single arrows represent implications

The connections between the various concepts developed in this chapter are illustrated in the figure.

Further extensions

An analogue to the Allais paradox in the context of state gambles is a problem known as the Ellsberg paradox. A ball is to be drawn at random from an urn containing red, white, and blue balls. It is known that one third of the balls are red but it is not known what proportion of the balls are white (or what proportion are blue). First, do you prefer the gamble U which is

$100 if red and $0 otherwise

to the gamble V which is

$100 if white and $0 otherwise?

Second, do you prefer the gamble X which is

$100 if white or blue and $0 otherwise

to the gamble Y which is

$100 if red or blue and $0 otherwise?

Pause and consider. If you prefer the gamble U to the gamble V then you should also prefer Y to X. To see why this is the case assign a utility of 1 to $100 and 0 to nothing, and write the probabilities which you assign to the ball being red, white, and blue as p, q, and r respectively (and note that none of these subjective probabilities need be 1/3). Now if you prefer U to V then the expected utility of U, which is p, must be greater than the expected utility of V, which is q. This implies that $p + r$ must be greater than $q + r$. Since $p + r$ is the expected utility of Y and $q + r$ is the expected utility of X this in turn implies that, if your preferences have the expected utility property, you prefer Y to X.

However, in an experiment a significant proportion of people claimed to prefer U to V and also to prefer X to Y. This means that the preferences of these people did not have even the state-dependent subjective expected utility property, or, equivalently, did not satisfy either the substitution condition or the continuity condition (in fact, the former). The cause of this seems to be that people prefer being given probabilities to having to infer them. Again, make what you will of this.

The Allais paradox concerns probability gambles, the Ellsberg state gambles. A third paradox, known as Newcomb's paradox but popularized by the philosopher Robert Nozick (1938–2002), concerns choice under uncertainty in general. You are faced with two boxes, one open and one closed. You have to choose either both boxes or just the closed box. You can see $100 in the open box; and you are told that a supreme being, who always predicts correctly, has placed $1m in the closed box if he has predicted that you will take only that box and has put nothing in it otherwise. Do you choose both boxes or just the closed box?

Nozick puts this problem to a large number of people and observes that 'To almost everyone it is perfectly clear and obvious what

47

should be done. The difficulty is that these people seem to divide almost evenly in the problem, with large numbers thinking that the opposing half is just being silly'. It would indeed seem that anyone choosing just the closed box is being silly: the supreme being has already placed or not placed the $1m so you might as well choose both boxes (as, after a lengthy analysis, would Nozick). However, you should formulate your own response. (In doing so you might like to reflect that the Nobel-prize winning physicist Niels Bohr (1885–1962) when asked why he had a good-luck horseshoe on his wall is alleged to have said 'It's not that I believe in it; but I'm told that it works whether one believes in it or not'.)

Summary

Choice under uncertainty involves choosing from gambles, both when probabilities are given and when they are not.

The substitution condition requires that if you prefer one gamble to a second then you prefer any mixture of the first gamble and some third gamble to a mixture of the second gamble and the third with the same weights.

The continuity condition requires that if you prefer one gamble to a second and the second to a third then there is some mixture of the first and third which you consider indifferent to the second.

The expected utility of a probability gamble is obtained by multiplying the utility of each prize by the probability associated with that prize and adding these numbers; preferences over probability gambles have the expected utility property if you prefer one gamble to a second if and only if it has a higher expected utility.

Preferences over probability gambles are rational, that is, satisfy the substitution and continuity conditions, if and only if they have the expected utility property.

The state-dependent subjective expected utility of a gamble is obtained by multiplying the utility of each prize in the state in which it is received by the subjective probability associated with that state and adding these numbers; preferences over state gambles have the state-dependent subjective expected utility property if you prefer one gamble to a second if and only if it has a higher such expected utility, and have the (full) subjective expected utility property if this applies when the utilities assigned to prizes are independent of the states in which they are received.

The impartiality condition requires that if you prefer one gamble to another in one state then you prefer it in all states.

Preferences have the state-dependent subjective expected utility property if and only if they satisfy the substitution and continuity conditions (as applied to state gambles); they have the (full) subjective expected utility property if and only if, in addition, they satisfy the impartiality condition.

Chapter 4
Gambling and insurance

As a digression from the main story I now turn to a special case of choice from gambles, that in which all prizes are sums of money. I shall for the most part present the discussion in the context in which probabilities are given rather than that in which they are not. However, in the light of the discussion of Chapter 3 the story can just as well be interpreted in the second context by replacing given probabilities with subjective probabilities.

Attitudes to risk

We can express gambles involving money either in terms of final wealth or in terms of gains and losses. For example, if your current wealth is $5000 then the gamble which gives you a final wealth of either $4000 or $6000 can be expressed as one in which you either gain or lose $1000. I shall use whichever form is the more convenient at the time, but shall distinguish the form in which prizes are expressed as gains or losses by preceding these with a plus or minus sign.

I shall, for reasons which will become apparent, assume that wealth can vary continuously. I shall also allow all gambles other than those which might reduce your wealth to some negative amount, however much these might increase your wealth. (We might note parenthetically that this implies that there are infinitely many prizes.)

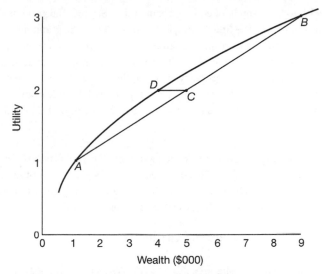

9. **A utility schedule: the expected value of the gamble which results in your wealth being either at _A_ or at _B_ with equal probability is your wealth at _C_, the certainty equivalent of this gamble is your wealth at _D_, and the risk premium of this gamble is the distance between _C_ and _D_**

Drawing on the theory developed in Chapter 3, we can assign a cardinal utility to each possible prize. If we take it that you start with some given level of wealth this is the same as assigning a utility to each level of wealth, or specifying a *utility schedule* for wealth. For example, your utility schedule may assign to each level of wealth (expressed in thousands of dollars) the square root of that level; in this case you would, for instance, assign a utility of 2 to a wealth of $4000. (I shall refer to this schedule as the square root schedule.) A utility schedule can be illustrated by a graph in which your wealth is measured on the horizontal axis and your utility on the vertical. Such a schedule (in fact the square root schedule) is illustrated in the figure.

The graph here has various properties. First, it slopes upwards: I shall make the uncontentious assumption that you prefer more wealth to less, which, of course, ensures this. Second, the graph is concave, that is, the line joining any two points on the graph lies entirely beneath the graph: I shall discuss this property, which is a matter of some substance, later. Third, the graph is continuous, that is, has no jumps. This property is an implication of the graph being concave: if you draw a graph with a jump you will be able draw between some two points a line which does not lie entirely beneath the graph.

I shall make use of two aspects of a gamble: its *expected value* and its *certainty equivalent*. The expected value of a gamble is obtained by multiplying each prize by its probability and adding the resulting numbers. For example, the expected value of the gamble

$9000 wp 0.2, $5000 wp 0.5, and $1000 wp 0.3

is, in thousands of dollars, $(9 \times 0.2) + (5 \times 0.5) + (1 \times 0.3)$, or $4600. (Expected value is analogous to expected utility. However, expected value only makes sense where all prizes are in the same units, such as dollars. If they were not then we could not in general multiply them by probabilities and then add them.) I shall call a gamble *fair* if its expected value is zero, favourable if this is positive, and unfavourable if this is negative. (Fair is used in the actuarial sense; it has no ethical overtones.)

The certainty equivalent of a gamble is the sum which you would accept in place of the gamble, or, equivalently, would pay to get the gamble. More precisely, it is the amount of money which, if you had it with certainty, you would consider indifferent to the gamble. It is easy to see that a gamble has one and only one certainty equivalent. (If we did not allow wealth to vary continuously, but only in steps of, say, $1, this might not be the case: it might well be that you considered $1000 to be worse than some gamble and $1001 better.)

To illustrate the calculation of a certainty equivalent, assume that your utility schedule is the square root schedule and consider the gamble which, if you take it, will result in your wealth either being $9000, in which case your utility is 3, or $1000, in which case your utility is 1, each with equal probability. The expected utility of this gamble is 2 and the certainty equivalent of the gamble is the level of wealth at which your utility is the same as this expected utility of 2, that is, $4000. This is illustrated in the graph above: the gamble results in your wealth being either at A or at B; your expected utility is your utility at C; and the certainty equivalent is your wealth at D.

I shall say that you are *risk averse* with respect to a gamble if you prefer the expected value of the gamble with certainty to the gamble itself; equivalently, you are risk averse if the expected value is greater than the certainty equivalent. Conversely, you are risk loving if you prefer the gamble to its expected value, or if the expected value is less than the certainty equivalent. The difference between the expected value and the certainty equivalent is the *risk premium* for the gamble. The expected value of the gamble which we have just considered, which will result in your wealth either being $9000 or $1000 with equal probability, is $5000; the risk premium is thus $5000–$4000, or $1000. This too is illustrated in the graph: the expected value of the gamble is your wealth at C; the risk premium is the distance between C and D.

It is clear that you are risk averse with respect to a gamble if its risk premium is positive, and risk loving if this is negative. I shall say that you are risk averse (without qualification) if you are risk averse with respect to all gambles, and risk loving if you are risk loving with respect to all gambles. It is easy to see that you are risk averse if the graph of the utility schedule is concave, and risk loving if this graph is convex (convexity is the opposite of concavity).

It appears that risk aversion is the norm. If you think that you are risk loving the following example (due to Daniel Bernoulli, whom we encountered in Chapter 3, and so named because it was first reported in the *Commentarii* of the St Petersburg Academy) may change your mind.

St Petersburg example

A gamble is resolved by tossing an unbiased coin as many times as is necessary to obtain a head: if it takes only one toss the prize is $2, if it takes two tosses it is $4, if it takes three it is $8, and so forth. How much would you be prepared to pay for this gamble; that is, what is your certainty equivalent? Pause and consider.

If the amount which you would be prepared to pay is less than the expected value of the gamble then you are risk averse, at least with respect to this gamble. Even though the number of possible prizes is infinite it is easy to calculate the expected value. The first row in the following table gives the number, n, of tosses it takes to obtain a head; the second row is the prize if it takes n tosses; the third row is the probability of it taking n tosses (which is just the probability of obtaining n specified outcomes each with a probability of 0.5 consecutively); and the fourth row is the prize in the second row multiplied by the probability in the third.

Tosses	1	2	3	...
Prize	+$2	+$4	+$8	...
Probability	1/2	1/4	1/8	...
Product	$1	$1	$1	...

Adding the amounts in the fourth row gives the expected value. As this is the sum of an unending series each element of which is $1 it is infinite. Thus, even if you, perhaps rashly, agreed to pay $1m for this gamble you would be risk averse. Pause again and consider what, in the light of this discussion, you would be prepared to pay? Casual observation suggests that a typical figure is of the order of $16.

Measuring risk aversion

Since risk aversion seems to be the norm I shall, from now on, assume it. Recall that the risk premium is positive, and thus that you are risk averse, if and only if the graph of your utility schedule is concave. Indeed, it seems plausible that the more concave the graph of your utility schedule, the higher the risk premium, and thus the more you are risk averse. This suggests that we may be able to interpret the degree of concavity at some level of wealth as your *risk aversion measure* at this level.

If we are to do this we need to be able to measure the degree of concavity. At any level of wealth we can measure the slope of the graph of the utility schedule. This is the vertical change, or change in utility, divided by the horizontal change, or change in wealth, for an arbitrarily small change in wealth (and is thus the same as the marginal utility of wealth). This slope changes as the level of wealth changes: if the graph is concave it becomes flatter, or, equivalently, its slope decreases, as wealth increases. The degree of concavity is measured by the proportionate rate of decrease of the slope, that is, the rate at which the slope decreases divided by the slope itself.

To illustrate the calculation of a risk aversion measure, assume that your utility schedule is the square root schedule. Then your utility at wealth levels around $4000 is (approximately)

$3999   1.9997
$4000   2.0000
$4001   2.0002

The slope of the graph of the utility schedule just below $4000 is 2.0000 − 1.9997, or 0.0003 and that just above is 0.0002. The rate of decrease of the slope is thus 0.0001; dividing this by the average value of the slope itself, that is, by 0.00025, gives the proportionate rate of decrease, or the risk aversion measure, of 0.4. (This is necessarily approximate as we are using dollar changes in wealth rather than arbitrarily small changes; there is also some rounding error.)

It remains to see how robust this measure is. The first point to note is that your risk aversion measure does not change if your utility is transformed in a linear way. This is because doubling, say, all utilities doubles both the slope and the rate at which it decreases, while adding 7, say, to all utilities changes neither the slope nor the rate at which it decreases.

A second point is that, obviously, the measure is positive at some level of wealth if and only if the graph is concave around that level. Only a little less obviously, the measure is positive for all levels of wealth if and only if the graph is concave (everywhere), or, equivalently, if and only if you are risk averse (without qualification).

Now consider how we might compare your risk aversion with mine. An obvious way to approach this is to say that you are *more risk averse* than me if I would accept any gamble which you would accept but not conversely. It is easy to see that this is the case if and only if your risk premium for any gamble is greater than mine. But is there any connection between your being more risk averse than me and our measures of risk aversion? There is: you are more risk averse than me if and only if your measure of risk aversion at all levels of wealth is greater than mine.

So far, then, our measure of risk aversion seems sound. To see where a problem might lie we need to consider what it means for one gamble to be *riskier* than another. Consider the following two fair gambles: X, which is

+$150 wp 0.4 and −$100 wp 0.6

and Y which is

+$400 wp 0.2 and −$100 wp 0.8

Suppose you take the gamble X and, if you win, stake $250 on the toss of a coin, that is, take the further fair gamble

+$250 wp 0.5 and −$250 wp 0.5

(If you lose in the gamble X you do nothing further.) Using the procedure for evaluating compound gambles discussed in Chapter 3 it is easy to see that this two-stage gamble is equivalent to the one-stage gamble Y. Thus the gamble Y can be seen as the gamble X with a fair gamble added: we can sensibly say that Y is riskier than X. More generally, one fair gamble is riskier than a second if the first is equivalent to the second with one or more fair gambles added.

We can compare the riskiness of gambles which are not fair by looking at their risky parts, that is, at their gains and losses relative to their expected values. More precisely, the *risky part* of a gamble is the gamble with all its prizes reduced by its expected value; it is, of course, a fair gamble. For example, the risky part of the gamble Z,

+$500 wp 0.2 and $0 wp 0.8

whose expected value is $100, is the fair gamble Y. Accordingly, as Y is riskier than X, we can say that Z is riskier than X. In general, one gamble is riskier than a second if the risky part of the first is riskier than the risky part of the second.

I can now return to the main story. Consider two gambles X and Y with the same expected value. If you are risk averse then, not surprisingly, you will always choose X rather than Y whenever X is less risky. So far so good. But now consider two new gambles U and V: U has a higher expected value than V, but is also riskier. If you choose U rather than V, and if you are more risk averse than me, then it would seem natural that I will also choose U rather than V. If the higher expected value is compensation for the extra risk for you then it should also be so for me. If V is a degenerate gamble then it is easy to see that this is the case. However, in general it is not the case.

We have, then, a problem. It seems that there is something unsatisfactory either with our measure of risk aversion or with our understanding of what it means for one gamble to be riskier than another. Which would you amend?

Some extensions

Gambling (in the colloquial sense) and insurance each involve taking on a gamble (in the technical sense). Gambling involves taking on a new gamble. If you bet $100 on red in a game of roulette then you take on a gamble X whose prizes are +$100 (if red comes up) and –$100 (if it does not). Insurance involves taking on a gamble which offsets an existing gamble. If you have a car worth $5000 which is at risk of being stolen then you have an existing gamble Y whose prizes are –$5000 (if the car is stolen) and nothing (if it is not). If you then take on a gamble Z whose prizes are +$4940 (if the car is stolen) and –$60 (if it is not) then you end up with the net (degenerate) gamble whose prize is –$60 whether your car is stolen or not. Taking on the gamble Z offsets your existing gamble Y: it is insuring, at a premium of $60.

If the roulette wheel has a single zero then there are 18 red slots and 19 non-red slots (the zero is neither red nor black) so your roulette gamble X has an expected value of (+$100×18/37) + (–$100×19/37), or approximately –$3. If the probability of your car being stolen is 0.01 then your insurance gamble Z has an expected value of ($4940 × 0.01) + (–$60 × 0.99), or –$10. Since all commercial roulette wheels have zeros, playing roulette in casinos will always involve taking on unfavourable gambles. (All organized gambling is on unfavourable terms: national lotteries are an extreme case, in which staking $100 typically involves taking on a gamble with an expected value of –$50.) Since insurance companies have costs, insuring will also involve taking on unfavourable gambles.

There is nothing irrational either in gambling on unfavourable terms or in insuring on unfavourable terms. However, it is easy to

10. Roulette: at Palm Beach

see that if you are risk averse then you will not gamble on unfavourable terms, though you may insure. Similarly, if you are risk loving then you will not insure on unfavourable terms, though you may gamble. However, casual observation seems to suggest that many people both gamble and insure on unfavourable terms: they buy tickets in national lotteries and insure their cars. If you buy a ticket in a national lottery then you must be risk loving; if you insure your car then you must be risk averse. How can you be both?

One resolution of this conundrum relies on the fact that you may be risk averse at some levels of wealth and risk loving at others. In particular, you may avoid risks when poor but be more prepared to take risks as you become richer. Recall that if you are risk averse then the graph of your utility schedule is concave and if you are risk loving then it is convex. However, if you are risk averse at low levels of wealth and risk loving at high levels then the graph of your utility schedule is concave at low levels and convex at high.

As an example, suppose that your present wealth is $5000 and your utility schedule is as follows:

$1000	2
$3000	9
$5000	10
$7000	11
$9000	18

First consider betting $2000 on a horse at the fair odds of 2 to 1. This gamble will result in your wealth rising to $9000 with a probability of 1/3 (if your horse wins) or falling to $3000 with a probability of 2/3 (if it loses); its expected utility is $(18 \times 1/3) + (9 \times 2/3)$, or 12. Since this exceeds the utility of your present wealth, which is 10, you take the gamble.

Now consider your insurance decision. You can insure your car, which is worth $6000, at a fair premium of $2000. Your certain wealth being $5000 means that your car is insured: you must choose whether or not to cancel your insurance. Cancelling involves taking on a new gamble which will result in your wealth rising to $7000 with a probability of 2/3 (if your car is not stolen) or falling to $1000 with a probability of 1/3 (if it is); the expected utility of this new gamble is $(11 \times 2/3) + (2 \times 1/3)$, or 8. Since this is less than the utility of your present wealth, which again is 10, you do not take on this new gamble; that is, you insure. Note that this shows that you may both gamble and insure on fair terms; it is easy to see that if the terms become slightly unfair you may continue both to gamble and insure.

This is illustrated in the figure, in which your present wealth is at A. The horse gamble would result in your wealth being either at B or at C and your expected utility being directly above your utility at A so you take it. The new insurance gamble would result in your wealth being either at D or at E and your expected utility being directly below your utility at A so you do not take it, that is, you insure.

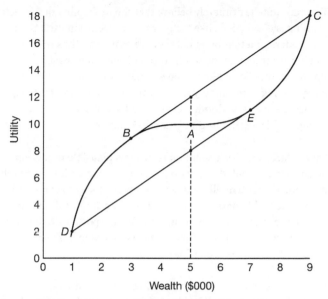

11. Gambling and insuring: if your wealth is at *A* you would accept the fair gamble which would result in your wealth being either at *B* or at *C* but reject that which would result in your wealth being at either *D* or at *E*

Ingenious though this resolution may be, it seems a little artificial. It requires not only that the graph of your utility schedule has the required shape but also that your present wealth is at the required level: it could not be much above that at *E* (or you would not insure) or much below that at *B* (or you would not gamble).

An alternative resolution is that people are risk averse at all levels of wealth and accordingly insure on unfavourable terms but do not gamble on unfavourable terms: they only appear to do so. If the odds against Alcove winning a race are 2 to 1 and you believe that the probability of his winning is 0.4 then you may well bet on him even if you are risk averse. This is because by doing so you are taking on the gamble which gives you +\$200 with probability 0.4 and −\$100 otherwise, the expected value of which is +\$20.

You may quite legitimately believe that the probability of Alcove winning is 0.4: beliefs, like tastes, are a subjective matter. You may well understand that bookmakers have costs, and thus that to gamble at random on horses is to gamble on unfavourable terms. But you may believe that you have some private information and are not gambling at random: you, and you alone, have caught the glint in Alcove's eye as he dominates the paddock. You will usually be wrong in this belief, but that is another matter.

On the face of it, this resolution seems less plausible in the context of gambling at roulette or national lotteries than on horses. Surely everyone knows that all numbers are equally likely to come up both at roulette and in national lotteries? You may know this, but the existence of numerous books and systems purportedly telling you how to win at roulette or which numbers to pick in national lotteries suggests that not everyone does.

I now return to the question raised in Chapter 3 of whether cardinal utility can provide a basis for arguments in favour of the redistribution of wealth. Recall that, although marginal utilities have no meaning when utility is ordinal, they do have some meaning when utility is cardinal. This is because if the difference between the utilities which you assign to $1000 and $2000 is greater than the difference between the utilities which you assign to $8000 and $9000 under one way of assigning cardinal utilities then it is greater under all ways. But what does this mean? It means that you are risk averse, no more and no less. In particular, it does not mean that there will be some sort of net gain if $1000 is transferred from someone with a wealth of $9000 to someone with a wealth of $1000. Apart from anything else this would involve an unjustifiable comparison between different people's utilities. More to the point here, it tries to read some sort of measure of happiness or well-being into what is simply a numerical way to represent attitudes to risk. Even if, ignoring the interpersonal comparison problem, we were to use cardinal utilities to justify redistribution, we would be redistributing simply on the basis of people's attitudes to risk. If people were risk loving then redistribution on this basis would take from the poor and give to the rich.

A more subtle attempt to justify redistribution uses an imaginary *veil of ignorance*. Suppose that everybody contemplates all the possible distributions of wealth. Some examples, for a population of 10 million, might be

1m at $1000, 5m at $4000, and 4m at $8000
1m at $1000 and 9m at $5000
10m at $2000

Not all distributions involve the same total as it is implicit that distributions have come about in some way which requires our participation and some distributions give greater incentives to participate than others.

Then without knowing his individual position in these distributions (that is, in the first distribution, not knowing whether his wealth will be $1000, $4000, or $8000), each person chooses a distribution. It is claimed that everyone will choose the distribution which gives the largest amount to the poorest person, or poorest group of people: in the present example everyone will choose '10m at $2000'. It is also claimed that the distribution which people choose from behind the veil of ignorance is just, and that if the actual distribution differs from this then redistribution is justified. This is the difference principle formulated by the philosopher John Rawls (born 1921).

> All social values – liberty and opportunity, income and wealth, and the bases of self-respect – are to be distributed equally unless an unequal distribution of any, or all, of these values is to everyone's advantage.

The first claim, that everyone will choose the distribution which gives the largest amount to the poorest person, is a substantive one and relates directly to choice theory. Behind the veil you have to choose from gambles such as

$1000 wp p, $4000 wp q, and $8000 otherwise
$1000 wp r and $5000 otherwise
$2000 wp 1

You will only choose the last of these three gambles if you are extremely risk averse. Indeed, if you preferred this third gamble to the second, say, for all values of the probability r you would violate the continuity condition. Thus the claim that each person will choose the distribution which gives the largest amount to the poorest person seems untenable.

The second claim, that the distribution which people choose from behind the veil of ignorance is just and that if the actual distribution differs from this then redistribution is justified, is a matter of ethics: choice theory will not illuminate it. However, I note in passing that there are other views. One is that a distribution is just if it is the result of voluntary actions and for no other reason. If you are wealthier than me because you are industrious and I am lazy that is the end of the matter: it is not for anyone to take from you to give to me. This is the entitlement theory formulated by Robert Nozick, whom we encountered in Chapter 3.

> We are not in the position of children who have been given portions of a pie by someone who now makes last minute adjustments to rectify careless cutting. There is no central distribution, no person or group entitled to control all the resources, jointly deciding how they are to be doled out. What each person gets, he gets from others who give to him in exchange for something, or as a gift. In a free society, diverse persons control different resources, and new holdings arise out of the voluntary exchanges and actions of persons. There is no more a distributing or a distribution of shares than there is a distributing of mates in a society in which persons choose whom they shall marry.

Summary

Attitudes to risk are manifest in choices from gambles in which all prizes are sums of money.

The risk premium for a gamble is (a) the expected value of the gamble, which is obtained by multiplying each prize by its probability and adding the resulting numbers, minus (b) the certainty equivalent of the gamble, which is the sum which you would accept in place of the gamble.

The risk aversion measure at some level of wealth is the proportionate rate of decrease of the slope of the graph of the utility schedule at this level.

You are more risk averse than me if I would accept any gamble which you would accept but not conversely.

You are more risk averse than me (a) if and only if your risk premium for all gambles is greater than mine, and (b) if and only if your measure of risk aversion at all levels of wealth is greater than mine.

Chapter 5
Conflict and cooperation

I now return to the main story and consider the case where menus consist of strategic items, which I shall now call actions, such as making a high or a low auction bid. This is the framework of game theory. However, I concentrate on how it might be rational for you alone to choose: game theory concentrates how we might each choose in a jointly sustainable way.

The setting

In a strategic framework you have to choose an action knowing that I, independently, am also choosing an action and that the outcome will depend on what we each choose.

Before proceeding, we need to consider the concept of common knowledge. Common knowledge differs from mutual knowledge. Something is mutual knowledge to you and me if we each know it; it is common knowledge if we each know it, we each know that we each know it, we each know that we each know that we each know it, and so forth. As an illustration of the difference between common and mutual knowledge suppose that you and I are each dealt a card. Each card is from a red suit but we do not know this: each of us sees only the suit of his own card. The dealer asks me and then you if we know the colour of the other's suit. Clearly, we each answer no. The dealer then tells us that at least one of the cards is from a red suit and repeats the question. Again, I answer no. But you, on hearing this, realize that my answer implies that my suit cannot be black; thus you deduce that my suit is red and answer yes. The point of this story is that your response changes, from no to yes, as a result of your being told something which you already know: that at least one of the cards is from a red suit. The reason for this is that the information which you receive turns mutual knowledge into common knowledge.

All the details of a strategy problem are common knowledge: the actions which we can each choose, the resulting outcomes, and the utilities which (drawing on the results of Chapter 3) we each assign to these. It is also common knowledge that we each choose rationally, in a sense to be developed.

As an example of a strategy problem, suppose that you and I are each to make an independent sealed bid in an auction of some wine which we each value at $100. To keep matters simple, only two bids are permitted: a high bid of $96 and a low bid of $94. After we have each submitted our bids the auctioneer opens them and gives the wine to the higher bidder, who then pays the auctioneer the sum which he has bid. If both bids are the same the auctioneer gives half the wine to each of us and we each pay the auctioneer half of the sum which we have bid. It is clear that your gain from each possible bid depends on what I bid, and conversely. If you bid high and I bid low then your gain is $100 − $96, or $4; if you bid low and I bid high your gain is $0, as your bid is not accepted; if we both bid high your gain is $0.5 × 4, or $2; and if we both bid low your gain is $0.5 × 6, or $3. My gains are similar. You have to choose whether to bid high or low.

The possible outcomes of the auction are set out in the table on the next page, in which the outcome '$4, $0' is that in which you gain $4 and I gain $0, and so forth.

	I bid high	I bid low
You bid high	'$2, $2'	'$4, $0'
You bid low	'$0, $4'	'$3, $3'

You and I each assign cardinal utilities to these outcomes. For example, we may assign the utilities

Outcome	You	Me
'$0, $4'	0	3
'$2, $2'	1	1
'$3, $3'	2	2
'$4, $0'	3	0

Thus you assign the utility of 0 to the outcome in which your gain is $0 and mine is $4, and so forth.

There are three aspects of this utility assignment which call for comment. First, you and I each assign utilities to entire outcomes, not just to our own respective gains: you may wish me well, and therefore, other things being equal, assign a higher utility to outcomes in which I gain more, or wish me ill, or not be concerned for me one way or the other. Second, utilities, being cardinal, already incorporate attitudes to risk. Thus if, for instance, you had the option of the gamble giving the outcomes '$2, $2' and '$4, $0' with equal probability you would, with the above utility assignment, be indifferent between this gamble and the outcome '$3, $3' with certainty as your (expected) utility in each case would the 2. Third, there is no suggestion that your and my utilities can be compared in any way: we each assign utilities independently.

We can combine the information contained in these two tables to obtain a *payoff matrix* for the auction problem. Specifically, we replace the outcome '$2, $2' with its associated pair of utilities, that is, 1 for you and 1 for me, and so forth. The rows of a payoff matrix correspond to your possible actions and the columns to mine. The entry for each row and column is the outcome, in the format of your utility followed by mine, if you choose the row action and I the column. We can now restate the Auction example as follows.

Auction example

You and I each have to bid astronomically high or boringly low in a sealed bid auction. The payoff matrix is

	A	B
A	1 : 1	3 : 0
B	0 : 3	2 : 2

The Auction problem is equivalent to the well-known Prisoners' Dilemma problem. In this problem you and I have been charged with committing a crime. We have been told that if we both deny the crime then we will each be convicted of a lesser offence and receive a light sentence; if we both confess then we will each receive a moderate sentence; and if only one of us confesses he will be freed and used as a witness against the other, who will receive a severe sentence. Before we can communicate we are placed in separate cells. You have to choose whether to confess or deny. Assume that we are each concerned only with our own sentences, and that we each assign a utility of 0 to a severe sentence, 1 to a moderate one, 2 to a light one, and 3 to being freed. Then it is easy to see that the payoff matrix for this problem is the same, apart from a change of names, as that in the Auction example.

Rational actions

Consider the following example (I shall not attempt to construct a story for this or for some of the following examples).

12. *The Game of Draughts*: the prize sits in the middle (Mattia Preti, c.1635)

Tree example

You and I each have to choose a tree: you can choose Ash, Beech, or Chestnut; I can choose Ash or Beech. The payoff matrix is

	A	B
A	0 : 0	3 : 1
B	2 : 1	2 : 2
C	3 : 2	0 : 3

You do not, of course, know which action or actions I will choose, or even with what probability I will choose each action. However, if you had been told these probabilities then your choice would be easy: you would choose the action which maximized your expected utility given these probabilities. This action is your *best response* to these probabilities. Suppose that, in this example, you had been told that I will choose A with probability 0.5 (and B otherwise). Then if you choose A your expected utility will be $(0 \times 0.5) + (3 \times 0.5)$, or 1.5;

if you choose *B* it will be 2; and if you choose *C* it will be 1.5. Accordingly, you choose *B*, which is to say that *B* is your best response to these probabilities.

Now assume that you are only told my *potential actions*, that is, the actions which I might choose. Attaching different probabilities to these will, in general, result in different best responses. For instance, if in the above example you are told that I will choose *A* with probability 0.2 rather than 0.5 then your best response will change to *A*, and if you are told that I will choose *A* with probability 0.8 then your best response will change to *C*. Your *plausible responses* to my potential actions are your best responses to some probabilities over these. In this example your plausible responses to my potential actions being *A* or *B* are *A*, *B*, and *C*.

Best and plausible responses can be used to explore rationality. An instance of a choice which would not seem to be rational would be that of your choosing *B* in the Auction example. What is wrong with this is that *B* is not a plausible response to either of my potential actions. Regardless of whether you are told that I will choose *A*, or will choose *B*, or might choose either, your only plausible response is *A*.

A more subtle instance of a choice which would not seem to be rational is provided by the following example.

Flower example

You and I each have to choose a flower: we can each choose Aconite, Buttercup, or Cowslip. The payoff matrix is

	A	*B*	*C*
A	1 : 0	1 : 0	2 : 1
B	2 : 1	2 : 2	1 : 3
C	1 : 0	0 : 2	0 : 1

Suppose that, in this example, you choose *B*. The problem here is less obvious. On the face of it your choice seems unobjectionable: *B* is a plausible response to my choosing either A or B. But you must ask yourself whether I would, in fact, choose A or B. Clearly I would not choose A as it is not a plausible response for me to anything which you might choose. Then might I choose B? If I did then I would have to believe that you would choose C, as my choosing B is not a plausible response to your choosing either A or B. But I know that you would not choose C as it is not a plausible response to anything which I might choose. It follows that you should know that I will not choose either A or B, and thus will choose C. But your choosing B is not a plausible response to my choosing C. Thus it would not seem rational for you to choose B.

A *rational action* is one which can be justified using a string of plausible response arguments, just as in the above example. In a strategy problem you do not know what I will choose. However, you may infer something about my actions as you know that I will only choose a plausible response. Specifically, you may infer that anything which I may choose will be a plausible response to whatever I infer you may choose. Further, as you know that I know that you will only choose a plausible response you should anticipate that I will make an analogous inference. Indeed, you should anticipate that I anticipate that you will make an analogous inference, and so forth. A rational action is one which emerges from this chain of reasoning: your action is rational if it is a plausible response to my plausible responses to your plausible responses to my plausible responses . . . Note that rationality is essentially an individualistic concept. In the Auction example we would both be better off if we each chose B rather than A: what is individually rational may well not be collectively rational.

We can illustrate this chain of reasoning in the Flower example with a table. Each row in this gives the person choosing, the other person's potential actions which the chooser is facing, and the chooser's plausible responses to these.

Chooser	Facing	Response
You	ABC	AB
Me	AB	C
You	C	A
Me	A	C

The chain comes to an end where neither your plausible responses nor mine change as the reasoning continues. This will clearly be the case if we reach a point where each of us chooses just one action, as applies here. We should note that we have started with your responses, rather than mine: however, it is easy to see that we obtain the same outcome if we start with my responses. Thus your rational action is *A* (and mine is *C*).

It is clear that you will always have some rational action. However, you may have more than one, as the following example (the original version of which is known as Meeting in New York) shows.

Meeting example

You and I have arranged to meet but have omitted to agree whether it is to be at the Anchor or at the Bear. As we each want to meet but do not mind where we can write the payoff matrix as

	A	*B*
A	1 : 1	0 : 0
B	0 : 0	1 : 1

If you had been told that the probability of my choosing *A* was greater than 0.5 then your best response would be *A*. If you had been told that this probability was less than 0.5 then your best response would be *B*. Thus, as your plausible responses are your best responses to some probabilities, your plausible responses to my potential actions being *A* or *B* are *A* and *B*. As my plausible responses are the same the rational actions for each of us must be both A and B (as, indeed, we should have expected from the symmetry of the example).

Undominated actions

To characterize rationality we need the concept of dominance. One of your actions dominates a second if, whatever I choose, you prefer the first; equivalently, your utility from the first is greater than that from the second. For instance, in the Auction example your action A dominates your action B. There is also a more subtle form of domination. Imagine that, instead of choosing some specific action, you could choose a combination of actions, or, equivalently, a gamble on your actions. This means that as well as choosing either X or Y you could choose the gamble 'X with probability 0.5 and Y otherwise'. A gamble on your actions dominates some specific action if, whatever I choose, your expected utility from the gamble is greater than your utility from the specific action. Consider the following example.

Insect example

You and I each have to choose an insect: you can choose Ant, Bee, or Caterpillar; I can choose Ant or Bee. The payoff matrix is

	A	B
A	0 : 0	3 : 1
B	1 : 1	1 : 2
C	3 : 2	0 : 3

In this example your gamble 'A with probability 0.5 and C otherwise' dominates your action B: whatever action I choose your expected utility from the gamble is 1.5 and your utility from B is 1. As this example shows, an action can be dominated by a combination even if it is not dominated by any of its components: your action B is not dominated by either A or C.

An action is *undominated* if it is not dominated by any combination (including any degenerate combination, that is, any action). In other words, your action is undominated if there is no action which gives you a higher (expected) utility whatever action (or combination of actions) I choose. As you might expect, an action must be undominated if it is to be a best response. Since it must be a best response if it is to be rational this means that it must be undominated if it is to be rational. However, the converse is not the case: an action may be undominated but not rational.

To see this, return to the Tree example, the payoff matrix in which is

	A	B
A	0 : 0	3 : 1
B	2 : 1	2 : 2
C	3 : 2	0 : 3

Here your action C is undominated but, as it is easy to see, is not rational.

The reason why your action C is not rational in the Tree example is that, although it is undominated, (a) it becomes dominated if my action A is deleted from the problem, and (b) it is reasonable to delete my action A because it is dominated (by my action B). This is to say that your action C does not survive the iterative deletion of dominated actions, or is not *iteratively undominated*: in other words, your action is not dominated by any actions of mine which are not dominated by any actions of yours which are not dominated by any actions of mine which are not dominated by any actions of yours . . .

For an illustration of iterative deletion return to the Flower example, the payoff matrix in which is

	A	B	C
A	1 : 0	1 : 0	2 : 1
B	2 : 1	2 : 2	1 : 3
C	1 : 0	0 : 2	0 : 1

In this we can iteratively delete actions as in the next table. Each row of this gives the person choosing, the other person's actions which the chooser is facing, and the actions which the chooser deletes at this stage.

Chooser	Facing	Delete
You	ABC	C
Me	AB	AB
You	C	B
Me	A	–
You	C	–

The process comes to an end where neither of us deletes any more actions. In this example your only action which survives is A (and mine is C). Note that the first time I choose I delete both A and B; it is easy to see that we reach the same outcome, though with more steps, if I delete only A or only B at this step. It is also easy to see that, just as in the process used to obtain rational actions, we reach the same outcome if we start with my deletions rather than yours.

The process of iterative deletion of dominated actions clearly has much in common with the process used to obtain rational actions. It is no coincidence that in the Flower example the two processes reach the same result: this applies in general. Thus we have a complete characterization: choice is rational if and only if it is iteratively undominated.

Although it might seem appealing we should beware of using what is known as weak dominance in place of dominance. One of your actions weakly dominates a second action if (*a*) whatever action I choose your utility from the first is no less than that from the second, and (*b*) for at least one of my actions your utility from the first is greater than that from the second. Consider the following example.

Bird example

You and I each have to choose a bird: you can each choose Avocet, Blackbird, or Crow; I can choose Avocet or Blackbird. The payoff matrix is

	A	B
A	1 : 1	0 : 0
B	1 : 1	2 : 1
C	0 : 0	2 : 1

In this example your action B weakly dominates (but does not dominate) both your action A and your action C.

We cannot iteratively delete weakly dominated outcomes with the same confidence as we can iteratively delete dominated ones. As our characterization of rationality tells us, iteratively weakly undominated actions are not the same as rational ones. Also, the order of deletion matters. If in the above example you delete A then I will delete A: you will choose either B or C and have a utility of 2. However, if you delete C instead of A then I will delete B: you will choose either B or C and have a utility of 1. None the less, if we have already deleted all dominated actions then it may make sense to avoid weakly dominated actions.

Sustainable actions

A question which arises is whether there is any connection between acting rationally and acting in a sustainable way. If we each choose rationally are our actions *sustainable*? And if our actions are sustainable must they be rational?

To proceed we need to consider what it means for our actions to be sustainable. I shall say that this is the case if your action is your best response to mine, and mine is my best response to yours. (A best response to an action is just the best response to the degenerate probability giving that action.) If this is the case then our pair of actions is sustainable in the sense that neither of us has a unilateral incentive to change. A pair of sustainable actions is also called a Nash equilibrium, after John Nash (born 1928), the Nobel prize-winning economist and mathematician (and the subject of the film *A Beautiful Mind*). Note that, although we can ask whether your action in isolation is rational, we cannot ask whether it is sustainable: sustainability is a property only of pairs of actions, one for you and one for me.

For an illustration of sustainable actions return to the Auction example, the payoff matrix in which is

	A	B
A	1 : 1	3 : 0
B	0 : 3	2 : 2

In this example each of us choosing *A* is sustainable, since if you know that I will choose *A* then you will choose *A*, and if I know that you will choose *A* then I will choose *A*.

As the Auction example suggests, and as follows almost directly from the definitions, sustainable actions are rational. However, the converse is not the case: not all pairs of rational actions are sustainable. The next example shows this.

Animal example

You and I each have to choose an animal: we can each choose Ass, Boar, or Cow. The payoff matrix is

	A	B	C
A	0 : 7	2 : 5	7 : 0
B	5 : 2	3 : 3	5 : 2
C	7 : 0	2 : 5	0 : 7

It is easy to see that in this example the only sustainable actions are

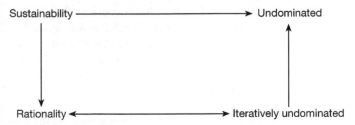

13. A map of strategic choice: double arrows represent equivalence and single arrows represent implications

your choosing B and my choosing B, but every possible action is rational for you (and also for me).

The connections between rationality, dominance and sustainability are illustrated in the figure.

My main aim in discussing sustainability is to investigate the connection between acting rationally and acting in a sustainable way, rather than to look at sustainability in detail. However, I shall briefly note two problems with the concept of sustainability.

The first problem is that there may be many incompatible sustainable actions. This can be seen in the Meeting example, the payoff matrix in which is

	A	B
A	$1:1$	$0:0$
B	$0:0$	$1:1$

In this example your choosing A and my choosing A is sustainable, as neither of us would choose B if he knew that the other would choose A. Similarly, your choosing B and my choosing B is sustainable. Thus we have more than one sustainable pair. This would not matter if your choosing your component of one pair and my choosing my component of another was also sustainable, but this is not the case: your choosing A and my choosing B is not sustainable.

A different interpretation of the Meeting example emphasizes this point. Reinterpret *A* as driving on the left and *B* as driving on the right; the payoff matrix remains unchanged. Then it is sustainable for each of us to drive on the left, and it is also sustainable for each of us to drive on the right; but if I drive on the left and you drive on the right we may not survive for long.

Note that there are no weakly dominated actions involved in either sustainable pair in this example: if there were then it might make sense to avoid them. Also note that the problem of incompatibility cannot arise with rational actions: you may have more than one rational action and so may I, but pairs of actions play no part in the story.

The second problem with the concept of sustainability is that there may appear to be no sustainable actions. This can be seen in the following example (the original version of which is known as Matching Pennies).

Matching example

You and I each have to choose and show a card bearing a picture of an Angel or of a Beast; if our pictures are the same I pay you $100, and if they differ you pay me $100. As we each like money we may write the payoff matrix as

	A	*B*
A	1 : 0	0 : 1
B	0 : 1	1 : 0

Clearly our each choosing the same action cannot be sustainable, for if I then knew your action I would change mine; similarly, our each choosing different actions cannot be sustainable, for if you then knew my action you would change yours. Thus there are no sustainable actions. This problem cannot arise with rational actions: as we have seen, you always have some rational action.

However, sustainable actions, of sorts, can be made to appear through the device of allowing gambles as well as individual actions to be chosen (as we did in the discussion of dominance). In this case a sustainable pair of actions, now sometimes called a Nash equilibrium in mixed strategies, has the same properties as before: your and my actions are sustainable if your action is your best response to mine, and mine is my best response to yours. If we allow gambles to be chosen then a sustainable pair of actions appears in the Matching example. It is easy to see that your and my each choosing the gamble 'A with probability 0.5 and B otherwise' is sustainable, and, indeed, the only sustainable pair of actions. In fact, if we allow gambles to be chosen then all strategy problems have sustainable actions.

Not only do sustainable actions appear where there were none, but new sustainable actions can appear in addition to existing ones. Recall that in the Meeting example, reinterpreted so that A is driving on the left and B is driving on the right, there are two sustainable pairs: each of us driving on the left, and each of us driving on the right. But if we allow gambles to be chosen then there is a third sustainable pair. This involves our each, independently, spinning a coin and driving on the left if it comes up heads and on the right if it comes up tails: another recipe for disaster.

If we interpret sustainability in this new sense it remains the case that sustainable actions are rational; again, this follows almost directly from the definitions. Also, not all pairs of rational actions are sustainable. To see this, return to the Animal example, the payoff matrix in which is

	A	B	C
A	$0 : 7$	$2 : 5$	$7 : 0$
B	$5 : 2$	$3 : 3$	$5 : 2$
C	$7 : 0$	$2 : 5$	$0 : 7$

It is easy to see that your and my each choosing B remains the only sustainable pair even when we can each choose gambles; however, as we have seen, every possible action is rational.

Thus the concept of sustainability may be ambiguous, as it is when there is more than one sustainable pair of actions; or empty, as it is when there are no sustainable actions and we do not allow gambles; or somewhat opaque, as it is when the only sustainable actions require the use of gambles.

Some extensions

The picture changes somewhat if time becomes relevant. Return again to the Auction example, the payoff matrix in which is

	A	B
A	1 : 1	3 : 0
B	0 : 3	2 : 2

and suppose that now we must each choose on two consecutive days rather than just once. On the second day we each know what we each chose on the first day. You now choose from the eight actions

A today and *A* tomorrow if I chose *A* today
A today and *A* tomorrow if I chose *B* today
A today and *B* tomorrow if I chose *A* today

and so forth. (My actions are analogous.) It is easy to see that your only two (equivalent) rational actions are '*A* today and *A* tomorrow if I chose *A* today' and '*A* today and *A* tomorrow if I chose *B* today'; that is, you choose *A* today and *A* tomorrow regardless of what I have chosen. Thus nothing essential changes.

Now suppose that we each have to choose on a hundred successive days. You may then feel that it might be worth your while choosing *B* on some of the early days in the expectation that this would build up some trust between us and that consequently I would start choosing *B*, which would be to our mutual advantage. However, you would be ill-advised to do this. On the last day the question of building up trust does not arise so we would each choose in the same way as we would if we were doing so only once, that is, we would each choose *A*. Then on the ninety-ninth day the question of building up trust would not arise as we would each know what the other would choose on the last day: again, we would each choose *A*. Repeating this argument, we would each choose *A* on every day. Again, nothing changes. The same logic applies if we choose on any finite number of days.

However, this logic does not apply if we choose indefinitely, as then there is no last day from which to start the induction process. In fact, if we choose indefinitely our each choosing *B* each day is not only individually rational but also jointly sustainable (although there may also be other sustainable outcomes). The picture has changed radically from the finitely repeated, and thus essentially timeless, case in which our each choosing *A* each day is the only rational outcome.

Generalizing from this result we may say that, while what is individually rational may not be collectively rational in a finitely repeated setting, it may (though need not) become so in an indefinitely repeated setting. Thus indefinite repetition may turn competition into cooperation. This result is such a part of folklore that it is known as the folk theorem. As David Hume, whom we encountered in Chapter 1, noted:

> I learn to do service to another, without bearing him any real kindness, because I foresee, that he will return my service in expectation of another of the same kind, and in order to maintain the same correspondence of good offices with me and others. And accordingly, after I have served him and he is in possession of the advantage arising from my action, he is induced to perform his part, as foreseeing the consequences of his refusal.

The tension between what is individually rational and what is collectively rational has led to much confusion. Some of this is encapsulated in the apparent paradox of the twins. The claim is that as the Auction example is symmetric you and I can be thought of as twins who will choose in the same way. As you know this you will bid low: you know that I will always do the same as you, and our both bidding low is better than our both bidding high. Attempts to justify the claim of symmetry are often based on what is known as the *Harsanyi doctrine*, after John Harsanyi (born 1920), the Nobel prize-winning economist and philosopher. This doctrine claims that two people with the same information and experiences will necessarily act in the same way. The doctrine, to which I shall return in the next chapter, is tautologically true if experiences are defined in such a way as to include everything that might make a person different. But then how relevant is it? You should take your own view both of this doctrine and of the apparent paradox.

In Chapter 4 I considered whether we could learn anything about distributive justice from the device of the veil of ignorance. I now turn to a similar device, the *veil of uncertainty*. The veil of ignorance represents a pretended lack of knowledge about facts which are already determined, such as who you are; the veil of uncertainty represents a real lack of knowledge about events which are yet to occur, such as who will find oil. Suppose that you and I are each prospecting for oil. We each start with zero wealth. If we both find oil, or neither of us finds oil, we each end up with the same wealth: the question of distribution is not very interesting in either case. Consider then the case where just one of us, we do not know which, finds oil; in that case one of us will have $2m and the other nothing.

I shall assume that we are each concerned only with our own gains, and are risk averse. To make the discussion concrete I shall assume that we each assign the utilities

$0   0
$1m   4
$2m   6

Before we set out, that is, behind the veil of uncertainty, we can independently choose to accept a redistribution agreement: whoever finds the oil will share the proceeds equally with the other. If we do this then, subject to one of us finding oil, we will each have $1m with certainty and thus a utility of 4. If we do not accept such an agreement, which will be the case if either of us backs out of the agreement, then, again subject to one of us finding oil, we will each have either $2m or nothing with equal probability and thus an expected utility of 3. The payoff matrix for this problem is then

	A	B
A	4 : 4	3 : 3
B	3 : 3	3 : 3

It is obviously rational for you to choose either A or B; it is equally obvious that our both choosing A is sustainable as is our both choosing B. However, A weakly dominates B for each of us so it may make sense for us each to choose A, and thus accept a redistribution agreement.

It is sometimes claimed that the fact that behind the veil of uncertainty everyone might choose to enter into a redistribution agreement supports the compulsory redistribution of wealth once the veil has been lifted. However, this claim seems problematic. An alternative interpretation of the claim is that it just makes the rather obvious point that risk averse people will freely choose to insure on fair terms. You should make your own interpretation.

Summary

Strategic choice involves your choosing from actions the outcomes of which depend on my choice as well as yours.

Your best response to some given probabilities over my potential actions, that is, over the actions which I might choose, is the action which maximizes your expected utility given these probabilities;

your plausible responses to my potential actions are your best responses to some probabilities over these.

Your action is rational if it is a plausible response to my plausible responses to your plausible responses to my plausible responses . . .

Your action is undominated if there is no other action which gives you a higher (expected) utility whatever action (or combination of actions) I choose; it is iteratively undominated if it is not dominated by any actions of mine which are not dominated by any actions of yours which are not dominated by any actions of mine which are not dominated by any actions of yours . . .

An action is rational if and only if it is iteratively undominated.

A pair of actions, one for you and one for me, is jointly sustainable if your action is your best response to mine and mine is my best response to yours.

If a pair of actions is jointly sustainable then each component of the pair is rational, but each component may be rational without the pair being jointly sustainable.

There may be many incompatible pairs of jointly sustainable actions, or none.

Chapter 6
Democracy and dictatorship

I now turn from the discussion of your individual choices to that of choices by a group of which you are a member.

The setting

A *group* is any collection of at least three people, such as a family, a club, or a nation: I shall concentrate on the group of travellers consisting of you, me and Montmorency. The group has to choose collectively from a menu of definite items: our particular group intends to travel together and has to choose from travel by Air, Boat, and Car. I shall assume that each person in the group is rational in the sense developed in Chapter 2. This means that everyone has preferences over menu items, and, indeed, can rank these. For example, our pattern of rankings might be

You	Me	Monty
A	C	ABC
B	B	
C	A	

Note that ties are permitted: although you and I each rank only one item top, Montmorency ranks every item top.

I shall consider how the choices of the group reflect the preferences of its members. The way in which members' preferences are taken account of in determining the group's choices is known as a *constitution* for the group; this specifies the choices which the group makes for every possible pattern of its members' preferences. There are two sorts of question we can ask about constitutions. First, do they combine individuals' preferences in an acceptable way? Second, are the choices which they specify satisfactory?

Acceptable constitutions

I shall start by exploring what it means for constitutions to combine individuals' preferences in an acceptable way. Perhaps the best known constitution is that of democracy, otherwise known as the *majority rule*: that the group chooses an item if at least as many people rank it top of the available items as rank any other specific item top.

An obvious example is the electoral system of 'first past the post'. If the left receives 40 per cent of the vote and the centre and the right each receive 30 per cent then the left is chosen. There is nothing obviously unsatisfactory about the majority rule as regards the way in which it takes account of individuals' preferences (though, as we shall see, it may have other problems).

However, other rules may not seem so acceptable. Consider the *Borda rule*, named after Jean Charles de Borda (1733–99), the naval officer and political theorist. This rule specifies that each person gives as a score to each item on the full menu the number of items which he considers to be worse than that item; these scores are added up and the group chooses the item with the highest total score.

In the electoral context this rule is referred to as (a form of) proportional representation. It was proposed by de Borda, against the violent opposition of Napoleon Bonaparte, that this rule be used in elections to the Academy of Sciences. To see why Napoleon may have been unhappy consider the following example.

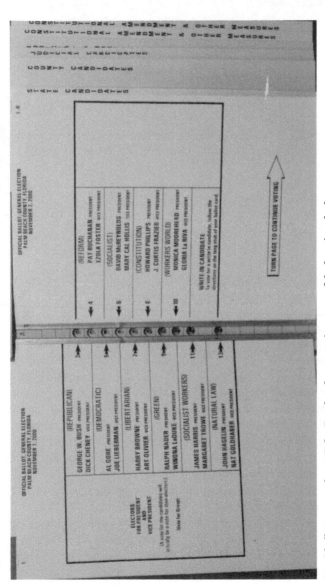

14. A ballot paper: also at Palm Beach – the mysterious case of the hanging chads

Borda example

We choose using the Borda rule. When our rankings are

You	Me	Monty
A	C	ABC
B	A	
C	B	

and we have to choose between A and C we choose A: A has a score of 3, C has a score of 2, and B has a score of 1. When our rankings are

You	Me	Monty
A	C	ABC
C	B	
B	A	

and we have to choose between A and C we choose C: C has a score of 3, A has a score of 2, and B has a score of 1.

The problem in this example is that the group choice between A and C changes when our rankings change, even though no person's preferences between A and C has changed: the choice between A and C depends on our ranking of the irrelevant item B. This seems unsatisfactory. For instance, if B is deleted from the full menu, say because of stormy weather, then the choice between A and C under each pattern of preferences in the Borda example differs from that when B is on the menu. (When B is deleted the choice under each pattern of preferences is both A and C: each has a score of 1.) To avoid such problems we might require that the group choice between any two items depends only on individuals' preferences between these two items. Equivalently, we might require that the group choice between two items does not change in response to any change of an individual's preferences which leaves his ranking of these two items unchanged. This requirement is the *independence condition*.

The independence condition would seem to be one of the minimal requirements for a constitution. Even if it is satisfied we may not be entirely happy.

Consider the somewhat trivial *alphabetical rule*: that menu items are ranked in alphabetical order and the group chooses the item ranked top of the available items. It is clear that this rule satisfies the independence condition. However, one of the problems with this rule is that it does not treat items symmetrically. Assume, for example, that everyone prefers U to V, and also prefers Y to X. Then the group will choose U from the pair U and V, but will not choose Y from the pair X and Y even though everyone ranks these items in the same way as they rank the items U and V. To avoid this problem we might require that if everyone ranks the items U and V in the same way as they rank the items X and Y, and the group chooses U from the first pair, then it chooses X from the second. This requirement is the *neutrality condition*. The neutrality condition is stronger than the independence condition. That neutrality implies independence follows directly from the definitions; and, as we have seen, the alphabetical rule shows that independence does not imply neutrality.

I now turn to potential problems of a different type. A further problem with the alphabetical rule is that it does not respect unanimity: the group will choose X from the pair X and Y even if everyone prefers Y to X. If we are to allow individuals' preferences to count at all it would seem odd if unanimous preferences, when they occur, were not respected. To avoid this problem we might require that if everyone prefers one item to a second then the group chooses the first alone from the pair. Note that we are not requiring that the first is chosen, let alone chosen uniquely, if the two are considered indifferent by even one person. This requirement is the *unanimity condition*.

This condition would seem to be one of the minimal requirements for a constitution. Even if it is satisfied we may not be entirely happy. Consider the *Pareto rule*, named after the economist Vilfredo Pareto (1848–1923): the group chooses an item if there is no other item which everyone prefers. It is clear that this rule satisfies the unanimity condition. To see what might be considered a problem with this rule consider the following example.

Pareto example

We choose using the Pareto rule. When our rankings are

You	Me	Monty
A	B	A
B	A	C
C	C	B

we choose both *A* and *B*. When our rankings are

You	Me	Monty
A	AB	A
B	C	C
C		B

we still choose both *A* and *B*.

What might be considered amiss in this example is that the group choice does not respond positively to changes in individuals' preferences. Items *A* and *B* tie under the first pattern of preferences, *B* moves up relative to *A* in my ranking while your and Montmorency's rankings remain unchanged, yet *A* is still chosen under the second pattern. To avoid this problem we might require that (*a*) there is some pattern of preferences under which each item is chosen, and (*b*) if one item moves up relative to a second item in one person's ranking while no one else's ranking changes then if the group originally chose the first item it continues to choose it, and if it originally chose both items it now chooses the first alone. This requirement is the *responsiveness condition*. The responsiveness condition is stronger than the unanimity condition. It is easy to see that responsiveness implies unanimity; and, as we have seen, the Pareto rule shows that unanimity does not imply responsiveness.

We have, then, four conditions concerning the way in which individuals' preferences are taken account of: neutrality and its weaker form, independence; and responsiveness and its weaker form, unanimity. I shall call neutrality and responsiveness the *strong conditions* and their weaker forms, independence and unanimity, the *weak conditions*. These four conditions together are consistent: it is easy to see that the majority rule satisfies all of them. Also, the two weak conditions are independent, as are the two strong ones. It is easy to find a rule which satisfies independence but not unanimity, and another which satisfies unanimity but not independence. Similarly, it is easy to find a rule which satisfies neutrality but not responsiveness, and another which satisfies responsiveness but not neutrality.

Reasonable constitutions

I have, so far, discussed only the first of the two questions we can ask about constitutions: do they combine individuals' preferences in an acceptable way? I now turn to the second: are the choices which they specify satisfactory? I shall approach this by asking whether the choices they make are reasonable, or rational, in the senses developed in Chapter 2. Specifically, I shall see if we can characterize the constitutions which satisfy various conditions and which produce reasonable, or, as the case may be, rational, choices.

Before doing so I shall, if only because it is so well known, digress briefly on the majority rule: that the group chooses an item if at least as many people rank it top as rank any other specific item top. As we have seen, the majority rule satisfies the strong conditions. It also satisfies a further requirement: that people are treated symmetrically; that is, that if two people exchange their rankings then the group choice remains unchanged. This requirement is the *anonymity condition*.

Indeed, not only does the majority rule satisfy these three conditions, it is the only rule which does this. We have, then, a complete characterization: a constitution satisfies the neutrality, responsiveness, and anonymity conditions if and only if it is the majority rule.

This characterization may be complete, but is it of any interest? The answer is unambiguously no. This is because not only may this rule fail to produce rational, or even reasonable, choices, it may fail to produce any choices at all. To see this consider the following example.

Majority example

We choose using the majority rule. When our rankings are

You	Me	Monty
A	C	B
B	A	C
C	B	A

there is no item which we can choose: two of us rank A above B so that we cannot choose B (either alone or with any other item); two rank B above C so that we cannot choose C; and two rank C above A so that we cannot choose A.

This is no small problem: recall from the discussion of Chapter 1 that to choose no item (as opposed to choosing an item labelled 'nothing' or 'status quo') is meaningless. Majority rule, then, may be vacuous. We must look further if we want a rule which is guaranteed to work at all, let alone to produce rational, or even reasonable, choices.

I shall start with the requirement that the constitution produce reasonable choices. We know that if we require group choices to be reasonable then we cannot also require the strong conditions and anonymity because the only rule which satisfies these is the majority rule, and this is not reasonable. We must, then, relax something. I shall first see what happens if we replace the strong conditions with the weak, then consider what happens if we abandon anonymity. (I shall not even consider abandoning the minimal requirements of the weak conditions.)

To see what happens if we replace the strong conditions with the weak return to the Pareto rule: that the group chooses an item if there is no other item which everyone prefers. As I have noted, this rule obviously satisfies the unanimity requirement. It is equally obvious that it satisfies independence and anonymity. But is it reasonable? Recall from Chapter 2 that choice is reasonable if for some 'at least as good as' relation the items which are chosen are those which are at least as good as every other item (and is rational if this relation is transitive). Under the Pareto rule there is indeed such a relation: one item is better than a second if everyone prefers the first; and if neither item is unanimously preferred to the other then the two are indifferent.

We might note in passing that this relation is not transitive, so that group choice is not rational. To see this return to the Pareto example, the (initial) rankings in which are

You	Me	Monty
A	B	A
B	A	C
C	C	B

Here we choose both *A* and *B* from *A* and *B*, and both *B* and *C* from *B* and *C*, but *A* alone from *A* and *C*. Thus the 'at least as good as' relation is

A is indifferent to *B*
B is indifferent to *C*
A is better than *C*

which is clearly not transitive.

However, the Pareto rule does produce reasonable choices, and satisfies the conditions. Indeed, the converse is also the case. We have a complete characterization: a constitution which produces reasonable choices satisfies the independence, unanimity, and anonymity conditions if and only if it is the Pareto rule.

To investigate what happens if we abandon the anonymity condition, but retain the strong conditions, I shall introduce the concept of a patriarch. You are a patriarch in some constitution if the group always chooses the items which you rank top of the available items, and chooses these alone unless everyone else ranks some other items top, in which case the group chooses these too. A constitution with a patriarch, who must necessarily be unique, is called *patriarchal*. The next example illustrates such a constitution.

Patriarch example

We choose using a patriarchal rule with you as the patriarch. Our rankings are

You	Me	Monty
A	C	B
B	A	C
C	B	A

When we have to choose from A and B we choose A, as you rank A top and the rest of us do not unanimously rank B above A; when we have to choose from B and C we choose B, for analogous reasons; when we have to choose from A and C we choose both A and C, as you rank A top and both I and Montmorency rank C above A. When we have to choose from the full menu we choose A, as you rank A top and the rest of us do not unanimously rank any other item top.

Note that in this example group choice is reasonable. The 'at least as good as' relation is

A is better than *B*
B is better than *C*
A is indifferent to *C*

However, this relation is not transitive, so again group choice is not rational. In general, the choices specified by patriarchal rules may be reasonable, but cannot be guaranteed to be rational.

We can now say what happens if we retain the strong conditions. The picture is bleak: any constitution which produces reasonable choices and which satisfies the neutrality and responsiveness conditions must be patriarchal.

If we require group choice to be reasonable, as surely we must, we have little leeway. If we want to retain anonymity (and the weak conditions) we have only the Pareto rule; if we want to retain the strong conditions we have only a patriarchal rule. The Pareto rule is unobjectionable as far as it goes, but it does not go very far: other than in the unlikely event of everyone agreeing it will always choose both items from a pair, which is not an enormous help. Patriarchal rules, on the other hand, go a long way: they will almost always choose just one item. But, if you were not the patriarch, would you want to live under such a rule?

Rational constitutions

I now consider what happens if we strengthen the requirement that the group choice be reasonable to the requirement that it be rational. If we are to satisfy this stronger requirement then we shall have to relax one or both of the strong conditions. This is because the only constitutions which satisfy the strong conditions and produce reasonable choices, that is, patriarchal ones, cannot be guaranteed to produce rational choices. I shall go the whole way and replace both the strong conditions with the weak: this leaves us with the absolute minimal requirements for an acceptable constitution.

To investigate what happens in this case I shall introduce the concept of a dictator. You are a dictator under some constitution if the group always chooses precisely the items which you rank top of the available items. A constitution with a dictator, who must necessarily be unique, is called *dictatorial*. It is clear that a dictator is a patriarch, but a patriarch may not be a dictator. An obvious example of a dictatorial constitution is that where group choices are always the same as your choices: as you are rational this rule produces rational choices.

We can now say what happens if we require only the minimalist weak conditions. The picture is even bleaker: any constitution which produces rational choices and which satisfies the independence and unanimity conditions must be dictatorial.

This result is known as Arrow's impossibility theorem, after Kenneth Arrow (born 1921), the Nobel prize-winning economist and philosopher. (It is called an impossibility theorem because it can be interpreted as saying that it is impossible to have all of the four properties: rationality, independence, unanimity, and non-dictatorship.) It is one of the most fundamental, and disturbing, results in choice theory. It implies, for example, that all talk of 'the national interest' is empty (other than in the unlikely event that everyone agrees, in which case it is redundant).

The connections between the impossibility theorem and the other concepts developed in this chapter are illustrated in the figure.

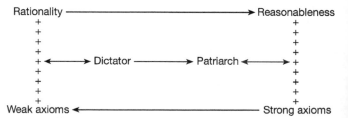

15. **A map of group choice: plus signs represent combinations, double arrows represent equivalence, and single arrows represent implications**

Because of the central role of the impossibility theorem, and also to demonstrate the type of argument which is used in choice theory, I shall, just this once, give a proof. If this is of no interest then you may safely omit it and go to the end of this section.

The proof has four stages. The strategy is to assume rationality, independence (this only implicitly), unanimity, and non-dictatorship and then show that a contradiction ensues; the contradiction implies that it is impossible to have all of these properties.

First, I shall define a set of people contained in the group to be *effective* over a pair of items if the group chooses the first alone from this pair whenever everyone in the set prefers the first and everyone else prefers the second. I shall show that if a set is effective over one pair then it is effective over all pairs. Assume that some set is effective over the pair U and V and consider the following rankings of four items by everyone in the set and everyone else:

Set	Else
X	V
U	Y
V	X
Y	U

Now the group chooses X alone from X and U because of unanimity; it chooses U alone from U and V because the set is effective over this pair; and it chooses V alone from V and Y because of unanimity. Then it chooses X alone from X and Y because choice is rational. Since everyone in the set prefers X to Y and everyone else prefers Y to X this means that the set is effective over X and Y. As X and Y are arbitrary the set is effective over all pairs.

Second, I shall define a set of people contained in the group to be *decisive* if, for all pairs of items, the group chooses the first item alone from a pair whenever everyone in the set prefers the first (regardless of the preferences of everyone else). I shall show that if a set is effective (over any pair) then it is decisive. Assume that some set is effective and consider the following rankings of three items by everyone in the set and everyone else:

Set	Else
X	Y
Y	$X \backslash Z$
Z	

where $X \backslash Z$ means that X and Z may be ranked in any way. Now the group chooses X alone from X and Y because the set is effective; and it chooses Y alone from Y and Z because of unanimity. Then it chooses X alone from X and Z because choice is rational. Since everyone in the set prefers X to Z and everyone else may have any preferences between X and Z the set is decisive.

Third, I shall show that, if a set of people is not decisive, then adding another person to the set does not make it so. Because a set containing only one person cannot be decisive, or that person would be a dictator, there are some non-decisive sets. Choose some such set and some individual not in this set and consider the following rankings of three items by everyone in this set, the individual, and everyone else:

Set	Indiv	Else
X	Z	Y
Y	X	Z
Z	Y	X

Now the group cannot choose Z alone from Y and Z because the individual is not decisive, so that it chooses Y, not necessarily alone, from Y and Z; and it cannot choose X alone from X and Z because the set is not decisive, so that it chooses Z, not necessarily alone, from X and Z. Then it chooses Y, not necessarily alone, from X and Y because choice is rational. Since everyone in the enlarged set formed by adding the individual to the original set prefers X to Y the large set is not decisive.

Finally, I show the contradiction. If we add an individual to non-decisive sets sufficiently many times we have, as a non-decisive set, the entire group. But the entire group must be decisive because of unanimity. This contradiction implies that it is impossible to have all of the four properties: rationality, independence, unanimity, and non-dictatorship. The proof is complete.

Some extensions

The most obvious criticism of the impossibility theorem is that it allows no role for 'intensities of preference': my preferring X to Y counts as much as your preferring Y to X even though having X means next to nothing to me but having Y is a matter of life or death to you. This is a consequence of the independence condition, that the group choice between two items X and Y depends only on individuals' preferences between X and Y. This condition has two components: first, that the group choice does not depend on individuals' rankings between either X or Y and some third item; and second, that it does not depend on any aspect of individuals' attitudes to X and Y other than their rankings, and, in particular, does not depend on any intensities of their preferences, or utilities.

We have already encountered the main justification for the first component in the context of the Borda example. In that example the choice between two items was seen to depend on what, besides these two, was on the full menu. But what is on the full menu is an arbitrary matter. Do we include travel by donkey if we are not sure whether any donkeys are available? Do we include travel using a technology yet to be developed? If so, how do we specify all the undeveloped technologies?

On the face of it, the second component seems unimportant: we know from Chapter 2 that preferences and utilities are interchangeable. Not surprisingly, the impossibility theorem continues to apply if we reinterpret it in terms of utilities without further restriction. But it would not apply if we could restrict utilities in some way which would make your and my utilities both measurable in some sense and comparable with each other, that is, if we could take account of intensities of preference. For example, the constitution could then specify that the group choose the item which maximizes total utility. It is easy to see that this choice would be rational, satisfy the unanimity condition and the first component of the independence condition, and be non-dictatorial. This approach to group choice is known as utilitarianism: 'the greatest happiness to the greatest number'. It was first proposed by the philosopher Jeremy Bentham (1748–1832). I shall return to this approach in the context of distributive justice.

The impossibility theorem is not the only disturbing result in the field of group choice. I shall briefly present two others. These involve liberalism and manipulation.

Liberalism implies that each of us should have some protected sphere. For example, whether you want to read Hume or Kant on the journey, provided that you promise not to discuss your reading with the rest of us, should be up to you. Let us replace the three menu items Air, Boat, and Car with the six items

Air and you read Hume
Air and you read Kant
Boat and you read Hume
Boat and you read Kant
Car and you read Hume
Car and you read Kant

Liberalism would imply that the choice between 'Air and you read Hume' (AH) and 'Air and you read Kant' (AK) should be up to you. More precisely, it would imply that you are decisive over such pairs, that is, that the group choice between AH and AK is AH if you prefer

AH, and *AK* if you prefer *AK*, with analogous requirements for choices between other relevant pairs. As a minimum, liberalism would give at least two people a protected sphere. (Note that even under dictatorship one person has a protected sphere.) I shall, then, say that a constitution satisfies the *liberalism condition* if there are at least two people who are decisive over at least one pair of items each. This is indeed minimal: only the smallest meaningful number of people is required to have a protected sphere, and each of their spheres is as small as spheres come.

The disturbing result is that liberalism is inconsistent with almost anything: there is no constitution which produces reasonable choices and which satisfies the unanimity and liberalism conditions. Note that only reasonableness, not rationality, is assumed, and that only one of the two weak conditions is required.

The second disturbing result is more practical in nature. It is well known that people may vote strategically in elections. That is, even if they prefer the left to the centre they may vote for the centre to keep the right out. Is such manipulation something to do with the particular electoral process, or is it more pervasive? Recall that a constitution is a specification of the way in which members' preferences determine the group's choices. Now that the possibility of manipulation arises we need an analogous concept. A *voting scheme* is a specification of the way in which members' reported preferences determine the group's choices; these reported preferences may or may not be truthful. A voting scheme is *manipulable* if, for some pattern of true preferences, there is at least one person who can obtain a better menu item by reporting preferences which differ from his true preferences when everyone else reports their true preferences. (Equivalently, a voting scheme is manipulable if everyone reporting their true preferences is not sustainable, in the sense developed in Chapter 5.)

The disturbing result is that effectively all voting schemes are manipulable: to be precise, every non-dictatorial voting scheme is manipulable. Note that not even the weak conditions are required: voting processes are inherently flawed.

All collective choices, then, must either be dictatorial or violate some very basic requirements; must be illiberal in the extreme; and must be open to manipulation. How should we respond to these bleak results? A libertarian response would be to make as many choices as possible individually, and choose collectively only when this is unavoidable. An authoritarian response would be to delegate power to a paternalistic dictator, a Platonic 'philosopher king'. A third response would be to concentrate on what is 'right', which does not depend on people's views, rather than what is 'good', which does. But these are just three possible responses. You should, as ever, formulate your own.

I shall conclude this section by noting that the formal framework of group choice can also be used to explore some aspects of individual choice. Suppose that you are to choose an occupation: Architect, Banker, or Cleric. There are various qualities which you look for in an occupation: income, flexibility, and satisfaction. You rank the possible occupations by their desirability according to each quality: for example,

Inc	Flex	Sat
B	C	C
A	A	A
C	B	B

You feel that your choice should satisfy two requirements. The first is that your choice between any two occupations should depend only on the various rankings of these two (the analogue of the independence condition). The second is that if one occupation is ranked above a second according to all qualities then you should choose the first (the analogue of the unanimity condition). Then the impossibility theorem tells us that if you choose rationally you will have to ignore all but one of the qualities (the analogue of dictatorship). Again, this is not a pleasing result.

Some further extensions

Nothing significant changes in a formal sense if time enters the picture. However, as regards interpretation, the introduction of time allows the possibility of a rotating dictator. The impossibility theorem tells us that the only constitution which produces rational choices and which satisfies the independence and unanimity conditions is that of dictatorship. But what is wrong with dictatorship? It is that the dictator can oppress everyone else. But what would happen if the dictator rotated indefinitely: if you were dictator today, I tomorrow, and so forth? You would be wary of oppressing me because you would know that I might later oppress you, and so forth. The folk theorem presented in Chapter 5 applies. In the context of strategic choice the folk theorem tells us that indefinite repetition turns competition into cooperation; in the context of group choice it tells us that indefinite rotation turns oppressive dictatorship into benevolent dictatorship. An example of such rotation is to be found in the constitution of the European Union, which specifies that the president, who has, in effect, dictatorial powers over the agenda, rotates according to a predetermined six-monthly cycle. Note that rotation is not a possibility in democracy: there are many possible dictators but only one possible majority. Under democracy it will always be in the interest of the majority to oppress the minority. An example here is to be found in bans on country sports.

I now return to the subplot of the distribution of wealth. We can, in a formal sense, express the question of distributive justice in the framework of group choice by interpreting the various menu items as different distributions of wealth. However, as a matter of interpretation, this involves some confusion between people's preferences and their values. Your preference may be to maximize your own wealth; your values may say that wealth should be distributed evenly. Group choices reflect people's preferences; distributive justice might be expected to reflect, if anything, people's values. However, if we do interpret the question of distributive justice in this way then the impossibility theorem tells us that there is no acceptable way to choose between different distributions: redistribution cannot be justified.

Whether or not we set the question of distributive justice in the framework of group choice there is clearly a connection between the two. As I have noted, the impossibility theorem would not apply if we could make use of utilities which were both measurable in some sense and interpersonally comparable. And, as we have seen repeatedly in earlier chapters, arguments in favour of redistribution rely, implicitly or explicitly, on utilities being measurable and comparable: we should redistribute from you to me because I am 'worse off' than you (Rawls's difference principle, encountered in Chapter 4) or because I would 'gain' more than you would 'lose' (Bentham's utilitarianism). As the economist Kenneth Binmore (born 1940) points out:

> If it were true that interpersonal comparisons of utility could not be made, I believe that there would be no point in writing a book about rational ethics. As Hammond, Harsanyi, and many others insist, ethics would then be a subject without substantive content.

Perhaps the most coherent attempt to derive measurable and interpersonally comparable utilities is the *ideal observer construction*; this is due to John Harsanyi, whom we encountered in Chapter 5. Imagine yourself behind the veil of ignorance introduced in Chapter 4, that is, in the 'original position'. You know what items are on the menu, but you do not know which role you will find yourself in. For example, you know that the group can choose to travel by Air, Boat, or Car, but you do not know whether you will be yourself, or me, or Montmorency. Behind the veil you have preferences over *item–role pairs*, that is, over conjunctions of items and roles. This means that you can compare 'Air travel while being yourself' (or *AY*) with 'Boat travel while being me' (or *BX*), and so forth: you may prefer *AY* to *BX*, or *BX* to *AY*, or be indifferent between the two. These preferences are your *empathetic preferences*. They are not the same as your personal preferences, which simply compare Air travel with Boat travel, and so forth.

Although you do not know which role you will occupy you do know what the possibilities are. Then, being rational in the sense discussed in Chapter 3, you assign probabilities to roles and cardinal utilities, representing your empathetic preferences, to item–role pairs. For example, you might assign cardinal utilities as follows:

AY 4
AX 2
BY 1
BX 0

We can interpret the excess of the utility which you assign to *AY* over that which you assign to *BY* as the extra utility for you of a change from Boat travel to Air travel, and so forth. In this case, the extra utility for you of a change from Boat travel to Air travel (which is 3) is greater than that for me (which is 2). This might reflect, for example, the fact that you suffer from sea-sickness but I do not. Further, as we know from the discussion of Chapter 3, the extra utility for you is greater than that for me however you assign cardinal utilities. It seems, then, that we have been able to compare your utility with mine in a way which makes sense.

However, we are not there yet. The interpersonal utility comparison we have made is your comparison: it is derived from your empathetic preferences. Montmorency's comparison might be entirely different: based on his empathetic preferences, the extra utility for you might be less than that for me. To overcome this problem we must resort to the Harsanyi doctrine, which we encountered in Chapter 5. This doctrine claims that two people with the same information and experiences will necessarily act in the same way. Behind the veil you and I have the same information, and are stripped of all experience. Accordingly, we have the same empathetic preferences, and thus make the same interpersonal comparisons. At last, we can compare your utility with mine in a way which makes sense. We can use this information to escape from the bonds of the impossibility theorem; and we may also be able to use it to justify the redistribution of wealth.

More precisely, we can say that total utility will be increased by a redistribution from those with a low marginal utility of wealth, usually taken to be the rich, to those with a high one, usually taken to be the poor, in the case where total wealth does not change as a result of this redistribution. (Whether this is provides any ethical justification is a separate matter.) However, we cannot as yet say anything about the more interesting case in which different distributions involve different totals, which would be the case if distributions have come about in some way which requires our participation and some distributions give greater incentives to participate than others. To say something about this case we must take the story further.

We must make two further assumptions. The first is that you consider each role to be equally likely. This implies that, if there are n roles, the probability which you assign to each is $1/n$. The second assumption is known as the *principle of acceptance*. This is that your empathetic preferences over those item–role pairs in which your role is that of me are the same as my personal preferences over the corresponding items: for example, you prefer AX to BX if and only if I prefer A to B.

Then behind the veil of ignorance you choose rationally in the sense developed in Chapter 3: you choose the item which maximizes your expected utility. In calculating this the relevant probabilities are the probabilities assigned to each role, and the relevant utilities are the utilities assigned to each item–role pair under the common empathetic preferences. Because of the first assumption these probabilities are all $1/n$. Because of the second assumption we can replace these utilities with the utilities assigned to each item under the personal preferences of the person in the relevant role. Then maximizing expected utility means maximizing total (personal) utility multiplied by $1/n$, which is the same as maximizing total utility. This is utilitarianism: wealth should be redistributed so as to maximize total utility.

An immediate criticism of this construction is that choices are observable, at least in principle, but preferences are not: you determine your preference between two items by asking yourself which of the two you would choose. It is not clear how you would, even as a thought experiment, choose between 'Air travel while being yourself' and 'Boat travel while being me'. Related to this, the Harsanyi doctrine is hard to justify. Why can you not prefer Air travel to Boat travel (for example, because it creates more employment) whatever your role, and I prefer Boat travel to Air travel (for example, because it causes less pollution) whatever mine?

We might also note that, even if redistribution from those with a low marginal utility of wealth to those with a high one were justified, this would not of itself justify redistribution from the rich to the poor. If the rich had a higher marginal utility (for example, because of an obsessive desire for luxuries, or, like Renton, an addictive need for heroin) this would require redistribution from the poor to the rich.

Further, even if the construction were sound, it would address what people choose, and possibly what is 'good', but not what is 'right'. The fact, if it were one, that it would increase utility does not of itself provide any ethical justification for taking from you to give to me. An alternative position is that which we encountered in Chapter 4: that a distribution is just if it is the result of voluntary actions, and for no other reason.

Binmore, who, as we have seen, is a supporter of the aims of the ideal observer construction, after a closer examination of this concludes that

> We have no choice but to rely on some measure of consensus already existing in the society under study if a common standard for comparing utilities across individuals is to be available. Harsanyi's brave attempt to argue that the circumstances of the original position create such a standard seems to me to lack all conviction when closely examined.

If there is 'some measure of consensus already existing in the society' then there is little need for interpersonal comparisons; if there is not, then the ideal observer construction seems to be of little help in justifying such comparisons. (We might note in passing that if Binmore is correct on both counts then 'ethics [is] a subject without substantive content'.)

You must take your own view of the ideal observer argument. If you are happy with it then the impossibility theorem loses its grip; also, redistribution becomes justifiable. If you are not prepared to swallow it then either you must find a better argument to justify interpersonal comparisons or accept the impossibility theorem and forget about redistribution.

Finally, note that the discussion of distributive justice in this book has concerned only the question of whether choice theory can provide any justification for redistribution. The fact that the theory offers little support for redistribution does not imply that there are no other arguments which might provide support (although, in fact, most serious attempts to justify redistribution have been grounded in choice theory). Further, the discussion in this book concerns only compulsory redistribution: it says nothing whatsoever about voluntary redistribution. To return to our starting point in Chapter 1, 'it is not contrary to reason for me to chuse my total ruin to prevent the least uneasiness of an Indian'.

Summary

Group choice examines the properties of constitutions, that is, the ways in which members' preferences are taken account of in determining group choices.

The independence condition requires that the group choice between two items does not change in response to any change of an individual's preferences which leaves his ranking of these two items unchanged.

The neutrality condition requires that if everyone ranks the items U and V in the same way as they rank the items X and Y, and the group chooses U from the first pair, then it chooses X from the second.

The unanimity condition requires that if everyone prefers one item to a second then the group chooses the first alone from the pair.

The responsiveness condition requires that (a) there is some pattern of preferences under which each item is chosen, and (b) if one item moves up relative to a second item in one person's ranking while no one else's ranking changes then if the group originally chose the first item it continues to choose it, and if it originally chose both items it now chooses the first alone.

The neutrality condition is stronger than the independence condition; and the responsiveness condition is stronger than the unanimity condition.

A constitution is patriarchal if the group always chooses the items which some specified individual (the patriarch) ranks top of the available items, and chooses these alone unless everyone else ranks some other items top, in which case the group chooses these too.

Any constitution which produces reasonable choices and which satisfies the neutrality and responsiveness conditions must be patriarchal.

A constitution is dictatorial if the group always chooses precisely the items which some specified individual (the dictator) ranks top of the available items.

Any constitution which produces rational choices and which satisfies the independence and unanimity conditions must be dictatorial.

Glossary

alphabetical rule: menu items are ranked in alphabetical order and the group chooses the item ranked top of the available items.

anonymity condition: this requires that if two people exchange their rankings then the group choice remains unchanged.

best response: your best response to some given probabilities over my potential actions is the action which maximizes your expected utility given these probabilities.

Borda rule: each person gives as a score to each item on the full menu the number of items which he consider to be worse than that item; these scores are added up and the group chooses the item with the highest total score.

cardinal utility: utility used in the expected utility property; equivalently, utility which retains its representational property only when transformed in a linear way.

certainty equivalent: the certainty equivalent of a money gamble is the amount of money which, if you had it with certainty, you would consider indifferent to the gamble.

compound gamble: a gamble whose prizes are also gambles.

constitution: a constitution for a group specifies the way in which members' preferences are taken account of in determining the group's choices.

continuity condition: this requires that if you prefer one gamble to a second and the second to a third then there is some mixture of the first and third which you consider indifferent to the second.

contraction condition: this requires that if you choose some item from a menu and this item remains available in a more restricted menu then you also choose it from the restricted menu.

decisive: a set of people contained in a group is decisive if, for all pairs of items, the group chooses the first item alone from a pair whenever everyone in the set prefers the first (regardless of the preferences of everyone else).

degenerate gamble: a gamble with only one (definite) prize.

dictatorial: a constitution is dictatorial if the group always chooses precisely the items which some specified individual (the dictator) ranks top of the available items.

distributive justice: the principles which determine what is a good, or right, distribution of wealth; for example, the principle that inequalities should be minimized, or, alternatively, that the distribution of wealth should be whatever emerges from voluntary actions.

effective: a set of people contained in a group is effective over a pair of items if the group chooses the first alone from this pair whenever everyone in the set prefers the first and everyone else prefers the second.

empathetic preferences: preferences over item–role pairs.

expansion condition: this requires that if you choose some item in pairwise choices with every other item on the menu then you choose it, though not necessarily it alone, from the full menu.

expected utility: the expected utility of a gamble is obtained by multiplying the utility of each prize by the probability associated with that prize and adding these numbers.

expected utility property: preferences over gambles have the expected utility property if you prefer one gamble to a second if and only if it has a higher expected utility.

expected value: the expected value of a money gamble is obtained by multiplying each prize by its probability and adding the resulting numbers.

explained by a preference ordering: your choice is explained by a preference ordering if it is explained by a preference relation which is transitive.

explained by a preference relation: your choice is explained by a preference relation if, for some 'at least as good as' relation, the items which you choose from a menu are precisely those which are at least as good as every other item on the menu.

fair: a gamble is fair if its expected value is zero.

group: a group is a collection of at least three people.

Harsanyi doctrine: the claim that two people with the same information and experiences will necessarily act in the same way.

ideal observer construction: imaginary choice from behind the veil of ignorance, knowing what items are on the menu and what roles exist but not knowing which role you will find yourself in.

impartiality condition: this requires that if you prefer one gamble to another in one state then you prefer it in all states.

independence condition: this requires that the group choice between two items does not change in response to any change of an individual's preferences which leaves his ranking of these two items unchanged.

item–role pairs: conjunctions of items and roles.

iteratively undominated: your action is iteratively undominated if it is not dominated by any actions of mine which are not dominated by any actions of yours which are not dominated by any actions of mine which are not dominated by any actions of yours . . .

liberalism condition: this requires that there are at least two people who are decisive over at least one pair of items each.

linear: utilities are transformed in a linear way when they are multiplied (or divided) by any positive number or when any number is added to (or subtracted from) them.

majority rule: the group chooses an item if at least as many people rank it top of the available items as rank any other specific item top.

manipulable: a voting scheme is manipulable if, for some pattern of true preferences, there is at least one person who can obtain a better menu item by reporting preferences which differ from his true preferences when everyone else reports their true preferences.

marginal utility: the extra utility assigned to an extra unit of wealth.

menu: a list of items from which choice must be made, set out in such a way that something must be chosen.

mixture: a mixture of the gambles X and Y is a gamble whose prizes are all the prizes of X and Y; the probabilities associated with the prizes of X are their original probabilities multiplied by the weight of X in the mixture, and similarly for those of Y.

more risk averse: you are more risk averse than me if I would accept any gamble which you would accept but not conversely.

neutrality condition: this requires that if everyone ranks the items U and V in the same way as they rank the items X and Y, and the group chooses U from the first pair, then it chooses X from the second.

ordinal utility: utility which retains its representational property when transformed in any increasing way.

pairwise: you choose an item in a pairwise choice with a second if you choose the first, not necessarily alone, when your menu consists of just these two items.

Pareto rule: the group chooses an item if there is no other item which everyone prefers.

patriarchal: a constitution is patriarchal if the group always chooses the items which some specified individual (the patriarch) ranks top of the available items, and chooses these alone unless everyone else ranks some other items top, in which case the group chooses these too.

payoff matrix: a matrix the rows of which correspond to your possible actions and the columns to mine; the entry for each row and column is the outcome, in the format of your utility followed by mine, if you choose the row action and I the column.

plausible responses: your plausible responses to my potential actions are your best responses to some probabilities over these.

potential actions: your potential actions are all the actions which you might choose.

preference ordering: a preference relation which is transitive.

preference relation: a specification of, for any two items on a menu, whether the first is at least as good as the second, or the second is at least as good as the first (or both).

preferences: preference orderings.

principle of acceptance: the claim that your empathetic preferences over those item–role pairs in which your role is that of me are the same as my personal preferences over the corresponding items.

probability: the probability of an outcome is a number, in the range 0 to 1, which quantifies how likely the outcome is.

probability gamble: a list of possible prizes with a probability attached to each.

rational (action): your action is rational if it is a plausible response to my plausible responses to your plausible responses to my plausible responses . . .

rational (choice): your choice (under certainty) is rational if it satisfies the revelation condition.

rational (preferences): your preferences over gambles are rational if they satisfy the substitution and continuity conditions.

reasonable: choice is reasonable if it satisfies the contraction and expansion conditions.

responsiveness condition: this requires that (*a*) there is some pattern of preferences under which each item is chosen, and (*b*) if one item moves up relative to a second item in one person's ranking while no one else's ranking changes then if the group originally chose the first item it continues to choose it, and if it originally chose both items it now chooses the first alone.

revelation condition: this requires that if you ever choose one item when a second item is available then whenever you choose the second and the first is available you also choose the first.

risk averse: you are risk averse with respect to a gamble if you prefer the expected value of the gamble with certainty to the gamble itself.

risk aversion measure: your risk aversion measure at some level of wealth is the proportionate rate of decrease of the slope of the graph of your utility schedule at this level.

risk premium: the risk premium for a gamble is its expected value minus its certainty equivalent.

riskier: one fair gamble is riskier than a second if the first is equivalent to the second with one or more fair gambles added; in general, one gamble is riskier than a second if the risky part (which is a fair gamble) of the first is riskier than that of the second.

risky part: the risky part of a gamble is the gamble with all its prizes reduced by its expected value.

state: a specification of everything which is relevant to your choice and about which you are uncertain.

state gamble: a list of possible prizes with, for each, a specification of the state in which it will be received.

state-dependent subjective expected utility: the state-dependent subjective expected utility of a gamble is obtained by multiplying the utility of each prize in the state in which it is received by the subjective probability associated with that state and adding these numbers.

state-dependent subjective expected utility property: preferences over gambles have the state-dependent subjective expected utility property if you prefer one gamble to a second if and only if it has a higher state-dependent subjective expected utility.

strong conditions: the neutrality and responsiveness conditions.

subjective expected utility: the subjective expected utility of a gamble is obtained by multiplying the utility of each prize by the subjective probability associated with the state in which it is received and adding these numbers.

subjective expected utility property: preferences over gambles have the (full) subjective expected utility property if you prefer one gamble to a second if and only if it has a higher (state-independent) subjective expected utility.

substitution condition: this requires that if you prefer one gamble to a second then you prefer any mixture of the first gamble and some third gamble to a mixture of the second gamble and the third with the same weights.

sustainable: a pair of actions, one for you and one for me, is jointly sustainable if your action is your best response to mine and mine is my best response to yours.

transitive: an 'at least as good as' relation is transitive if when X is at least as good as Y, and Y is at least as good as Z, then X is at least as good as Z.

unanimity condition: this requires that if everyone prefers one item to a second then the group chooses the first alone from the pair.

undominated: your action is undominated if there is no other action which gives you a higher (expected) utility whatever action (or combination of actions) I choose.

utility: utilities are numbers assigned to items in such a way that one item has a greater utility than a second if and only if the first is better than the second.

utility maximizing: your choice is utility maximizing if, for some assignment of utilities, the items which you choose are precisely those whose utility is at least as great as that of every other item.

utility schedule: a utility schedule for wealth assigns a utility to each level of wealth.

veil of ignorance: the veil of ignorance represents a pretended lack of knowledge about facts which are already determined, in particular, which position or role you occupy.

veil of uncertainty: the veil of uncertainty represents a real lack of knowledge about events which are yet to occur, such as what your wealth will be.

voting scheme: a voting scheme for a group specifies the way in which members' reported (but not necessarily true) preferences are taken account of in determining the group's choices.

weak conditions: the independence and unanimity conditions.

Further reading

Non-technical overviews of choice theory are provided by Elster and by Hargreaves Heap *et al.*; an overview of the subplot of distributive justice is provided by Roemer. Further reading relating to individual chapters is given below.

Preface
The Einstein quotation is from pp. ix–x.

Chapter 1
The concept of rational choice begins with Aristotle; the origin of its more formal treatment may be ascribed, more arbitrarily, to Robbins. The *Trainspotting* quotations are from pp. 3–5 and from p. 106 of Hodge (with each occurrence of 'fucking' omitted); the Aristotle quotations are from p. 139; and the Hume quotations are from pp. 266–7 (with abbreviations completed and emphasis omitted).

Chapter 2
The formal treatment of choice under certainty originates with Samuelson. Proofs of all the claims made in the main discussion may be found in Fishburn (chapters 2 and 3) or in Suzumura (chapter 2).

Chapter 3
The formal treatment of choice where probabilities are given originates with von Neumann and Morgenstern; that where probabilities must be

inferred originates with Savage, or, in the framework employed in this chapter, with Anscombe and Aumann. The Nozick quotation is from *Socratic Puzzles*, p. 48. Proofs of all the claims made in the main discussion may be found in Fishburn (chapters 8 and 12) or in Kreps (chapters 5 and 7); those relating to the case where probabilities are not given involve some serious mathematics.

Chapter 4

The formal treatment of risk aversion originates with Pratt. The Rawls quotation is from p. 62; and the Nozick quotation is from *Anarchy*, pp. 149–50 (with emphasis omitted). Proofs of all the claims made in the main discussion may be found in Arrow's *Essays* (chapter 3) or in Kreps (chapter 6); those relating to the measure of risk aversion involve some serious mathematics.

Chapter 5

The formal treatment of individual rationality in a strategic setting originates with Bernheim and with Pearce; that of jointly sustainable choice in such a setting originates with Nash. The Hume quotation is from pp. 334–5 (with abbreviations completed). Proofs of all the claims made in the main discussion may be found in Fudenberg and Tirole (chapters 1 and 2) or in Osborne and Rubinstein (chapters 2 and 4); those relating to the equivalence between strategic rationality and freedom from iterative dominance, and to the existence of mixed strategy equilibria, involve some serious mathematics.

Chapter 6

The formal treatment of group choice originates with Arrow's *Social Choice*. The Binmore quotations are from pp. 283 and 300 (with references and emphasis omitted). The proof of the impossibility theorem follows that of Allingham, pp. 23–5. Proofs of all the claims made in the main discussion may be found in Sen (chapters 3*–6*) or in Suzumura (chapters 3–7).

References

M. Allingham, *Value* (Macmillan, 1983).

F. J. Anscombe and R. J. Aumann, 'A Definition of Subjective
Probability', *Annals of Mathematical Statistics*, 34 (1963),
199–205.

Aristotle, *The Nicomachean Ethics*, tr. D. Ross, rev. J. L. Ackrill and
J. O. Urmson (Oxford University Press, 1998).

K. J. Arrow, *Essays in the Theory of Risk Bearing* (North
Holland, 1974).

—— *Social Choice and Individual Values* (Wiley, 1951).

B. D. Bernheim, 'Rationalizable Strategic Behavior', *Econometrica*,
52 (1984), 1007–28.

K. G. Binmore, *Playing Fair* (MIT Press, 1994).

A. Einstein, *Relativity*, tr. R. W. Lawson (Routledge, 2001).

J. Elster (ed.), *Rational Choice* (Blackwell, 1986).

P. C. Fishburn, *Utility Theory for Decision Making* (Wiley, 1970).

J. Fudenberg and J. Tirole, *Game Theory* (MIT Press, 1991).

S. Hargreaves Heap, M. Hollis, B. Lyons, R. Sugden, and A. Weale,
The Theory of Choice: A Critical Guide (Blackwell, 1992).

J. Hodge, *Trainspotting* (Faber & Faber, 1996).

D. Hume, *A Treatise of Human Nature*, ed. D. F. and M. J. Norton
(Oxford University Press, 2000).

D. M. Kreps, *Notes on the Theory of Choice* (Westview, 1988).

J. F. Nash, 'Non-cooperative Games', *Annals of Mathematics*, 54
(1951), 286–95.

J. von Neumann and O. Morgenstern, *The Theory of Games and Economic Behavior* (Princeton University Press, 1944).

R. Nozick, *Anarchy, State, and Utopia* (Basil Blackwell, 1974).

—— *Socratic Puzzles* (Harvard University Press, 1997).

M. J. Osborne and A. Rubinstein, *A Course in Game Theory* (MIT Press, 1994).

D. G. Pearce, 'Rationalizable Strategic Behavior and the Problem of Perfection', *Econometrica*, 52 (1984), 1029–50.

R. W. Pratt, 'Risk Aversion in the Small and in the Large', *Econometrica*, 32 (1964), 122–36.

J. Rawls, *A Theory of Justice* (Oxford University Press, 1972).

L. Robbins, *An Essay on the Nature and Significance of Economic Science* (Macmillan, 1932).

J. E. Roemer, *Theories of Distributive Justice* (Harvard University Press, 1996).

P. A. Samuelson, *Foundations of Economic Analysis* (Harvard University Press, 1947).

L. J. Savage, *Foundations of Statistics* (Wiley, 1954).

A. K. Sen, *Collective Choice and Social Welfare* (Oliver & Boyd, 1970).

K. Suzumura, *Rational Choice, Collective Decisions, and Social Welfare* (Cambridge University Press, 1983).

Index

Expand your collection of
VERY SHORT INTRODUCTIONS

Visit the
VERY SHORT
INTRODUCTIONS
Web site

www.oup.co.uk/vsi

➤ **Information** about all published titles

➤ News of **forthcoming books**

➤ **Extracts** from the books, including titles not yet published

➤ **Reviews** and views

➤ **Links** to other **web sites** and main OUP web page

➤ Information about **VSIs in translation**

➤ **Contact** the editors

➤ **Order** other **VSIs** on-line

MUSIC
A Very Short Introduction
Nicholas Cook

This stimulating Very Short Introduction to music
invites us to really *think* about music and the values
and qualities we ascribe to it.

'A *tour de force*. Nicholas Cook is without doubt one of
the most probing and creative thinkers about music we
have today.'
Jim Samson, University of Bristol

'Nicholas Cook offers a perspective that is clearly influ-
enced by recent writing in a host of disciplines related
to music. It may well prove a landmark in the appreci-
ation of the topic … In short, I can hardly imagine it being
done better.'
Roger Parker, University of Cambridge

www.oup.co.uk/vsi/music

BUDDHISM
A Very Short Introduction
Damien Keown

From its origin in India over two thousand years
ago Buddhism has spread throughout Asia and is now
exerting an increasing influence on western culture. In
clear and straightforward language, and with the help of
maps, diagrams and illustrations, this book explains how
Buddhism began and how it evolved into its present-day
form. The central teachings and practices are set out
clearly, and keys topics such as karma and rebirth, medi-
tation, ethics, and Buddhism in the West receive detailed
coverage in separate chapters. The distinguishing fea-
tures of the main schools – such as Tibetan and Zen
Buddhism – are clearly explained. The book will be
of interest to anyone seeking a sound basic
understanding of Buddhism.

> 'Damien Keown's book is a readable and wonderfully
> lucid introduction to one of mankind's most beautiful,
> profound, and compelling systems of wisdom. His
> impressive powers of explanation help us to come to
> terms with a vital contemporary reality.'
>
> **Bryan Appleyard**

www.oup.co.uk/vsi/buddhism

LITERARY THEORY
A Very Short Introduction
Jonathan Culler

Literary Theory is a controversial subject. Said to have transformed the study of culture and society in the past two decades, it is accused of undermining respect for tradition and truth, encouraging suspicion about the political and psychological implications of cultural products instead of admiration for great literature. In this Very Short Introduction, Jonathan Culler explains 'theory', not by describing warring 'schools' but by sketching key 'moves' that theory has encouraged and speaking directly about the implications of cultural theory for thinking about literature, about the power of language, and about human identity. This lucid introduction will be useful for anyone who has wondered what all the fuss is about or who wants to think about literature today.

> 'It is impossible to imagine a clearer treatment of the subject, or one that is, within the given limits of length, more comprehensive. Culler has always been remarkable for his expository skills, and here he has found exactly the right method and tone for his purposes.'
>
> **Frank Kermode**

www.oup.co.uk/vsi/literarytheory